FREEWAY

A NOT-SO-PERFECT GUIDE TO FREEDOM

MIKE FOSTER

GARRY POOLE

FOR EVERY ACHING HEART NEEDING
TO KNOW GOD'S LOVE AND GRACE:
THIS IS FOR YOU.

START HERE

WRITE YOUR FULL NAME ON THIS LINE:

WRITE YOUR NICKNAME THAT YOUR FRIENDS CALL YOU ON THIS LINE:

WRITE THE NAME OF YOUR FAVORITE DRINK AT STARBUCKS:

YOUR PHONE NUMBER:

LOST AND FOUND

IF SOMEONE FINDS YOUR BOOK, DO YOU WANT THEM TO CALL THAT NUMBER?

 YES! CALL ME!   NO, JUST KEEP IT.

OR EMAIL ME AT:

CREATE YOUR MY FREEWAY ACCOUNT TODAY!

LOG ON TO SECONDCHANCE.ORG/MYFREEWAY

SIGN UP FOR YOUR FREE ACCOUNT.

(IT TAKES 20 SECONDS)

ACCESS OUR DAILY DEVOTIONS, PREMIUM CONTENT AND VIDEOS.

LET THE AWESOMENESS BEGIN.

A Note From Mike

Hello!

I'm thrilled you're going through what my friends and I experienced just over a year ago. This entire *Freeway* thing started with us having a basic belief that we could share our struggles and find freedom in God's grace. Together, we dreamed about creating something that would help everyone find the way to be free.

In October and November of 2012 we met at my house on Monday nights and experimented with what you're about to go through. Those nights were awesome, jumbled, awkward, and exhilarating. We worked through some simple questions and passages from the Bible and shared our stories of struggle. We ate cheesecake, nibbled on finger foods, and listened like friends should listen.

On the night we talked about forgiveness, we met at Ponto Beach and froze to death around an inadequate campfire. On our final evening we feasted like kings and queens at Buca di Beppo and enjoyed one another's warm company. Great memories were made on those Monday nights we spent together.

God did something remarkable through those genuine conversations. Grace was finally setting us free, and we were finding a breakthrough. And though we didn't know what it all meant, we desperately wanted others to join us on this not-so-perfect journey to freedom.

In these coming weeks, you will be going on a similar soul adventure. It will involve getting honest with yourself and having your own authentic conversations with friends. It will be really hard but totally worth it. In the days ahead you will experience the miracle of how God takes broken things and makes them beautiful again.

Cheering you on,

Mike Foster

CONTENTS

WHAT IS FREEWAY? - 6

HOW TO USE THIS BOOK - 8

FREEWAY: THE STORY OF FRIENDS - - - - - - - - - - - - - - - - - 14

INTRO: A PRODIGAL'S PARTY

PREPARE - 24

EXPLORE - 30

SHARE - 36

JUMP IN - 41

REMEMBER - 42

STEP 1: AWARENESS

PREPARE - 48

EXPLORE - 54

SHARE - 70

JUMP IN - 73

REMEMBER - 74

STEP 2: DISCOVERY

PREPARE - 80

EXPLORE - 84

SHARE - 100

JUMP IN - 103

REMEMBER - 104

STEP 3: OWNERSHIP

PREPARE - 110

EXPLORE - 114

STEP 3: CONTINUED

SHARE - 124

JUMP IN - 127

REMEMBER - 128

STEP 4: FORGIVENESS

PREPARE - 134

EXPLORE - 138

SHARE - 150

JUMP IN - 153

REMEMBER - 154

STEP 5: ACCEPTANCE

PREPARE - 160

EXPLORE - 164

SHARE - 186

JUMP IN - 189

REMEMBER - 190

STEP 6: FREEDOM

PREPARE - 196

EXPLORE - 200

SHARE - 210

JUMP IN - 213

REMEMBER - 214

WHAT
IS
FREEWAY

QUITE SIMPLY, *FREEWAY* IS A WAY
TO BE FREE.

IT'S A GUIDE BUILT UPON GOD'S AMAZING
GRACE, CONVERSATIONS WITH FRIENDS,
AND AN HONEST EXPLORATION OF OUR
NOT-SO-PERFECT STORIES.

THROUGH THE PROCESS OF AWARENESS,
DISCOVERY, OWNERSHIP, FORGIVENESS,
ACCEPTANCE, AND FREEDOM, WE BELIEVE
OUR HEARTS CAN BE HEALED.

HOW TO USE THIS BOOK

1. PREPARE

These are short introductions to the big ideas of each step. They will help point your thoughts in the right direction and prepare your heart for the journey.

2. EXPLORE

These exercises provide a fun way to explore your not-so-perfect story and prepares you for your group time.

3. SHARE

Meet with your group and talk about what you are learning. Discuss the group questions together.

4. JUMP IN

These simple life experiments help you apply what you're learning and move ideas into action.

5. REMEMBER

Write whatever you want on these pages. Use this space to capture your additional thoughts or things that matter to you.

TIPS AND SUGGESTIONS

1. HAVE A REAL DESIRE TO CHANGE SOMETHING IN YOUR LIFE.

2. THE MOST BENEFICIAL PARTS OF *FREEWAY* HAPPEN WHEN YOU TALK WITH YOUR FRIENDS ABOUT WHAT YOU'RE LEARNING. SHARE GENEROUSLY AND WITH COURAGE.

3. BE FIERCE IN PURSUING THE TRUTH IN YOUR LIFE.

4. MARK THIS BOOK UP. SCRIBBLE STUFF. DRAW AND DOODLE. BEND PAGES. NO BONUS POINTS FOR CLEAN AND PRETTY PAGES.

5. CREATE A RELAXING AND UNINTERRUPTED SPOT TO DO THE EXERCISES. TAKE YOUR TIME. DON'T RUSH.

6. DON'T BE MEAN TO YOURSELF. BE HONEST AND COMPASSIONATE.

7. YOUR BRAIN WILL GIVE YOU TEN THOUSAND REASONS TO QUIT. DON'T LISTEN. IT'S AN EVIL TRICK.

8. YOU WILL GET OUT OF THIS EXPERIENCE WHAT YOU PUT INTO IT. SHOW UP WITH YOUR WHOLE HEART!

GROUP LEADER TIPS

1. ORGANIZE THE TIME AND GROUP LOCATION. INVITE YOUR FRIENDS TO BE A PART OF YOUR GROUP.

2. SET A COMFORTABLE, WELCOMING AND RELAXED ATMOSPHERE FOR EVERYONE. SERIOUSLY, HAVE LOTS OF FUN!

3. PUT TOGETHER ALL THE ITEMS AND MATERIALS THAT ARE NEEDED FOR THE GROUP SESSIONS.

4. LOOK FOR SOME WAYS TO SHARE THE RESPONSIBILITIES WITH OTHER GROUP MEMBERS.

5. BE RESPONSIBLE FOR STARTING AND ENDING ON TIME. THIS IS VERY IMPORTANT.

6. BE PREPARED AND FAMILIAR WITH THE GROUP QUESTIONS THAT WILL BE DISCUSSED IN THE SESSION.

7. IT IS A GOOD IDEA TO HAVE YOUR GROUP REVIEW THE "GROUP PROMISE" (PAGE 38) EVERY TIME YOU MEET.

TO WATCH GROUP LEADER TRAINING VIDEOS AND FOR OTHER LEADER RESOURCES, GO TO SECONDCHANCE.ORG/MYFREEWAY

FREEWAY GROUP DISCUSSION VIDEOS

OPTION #1: WATCH ONLINE

CREATE A FREE ACCOUNT AND STREAM THE GROUP
VIDEOS ONLINE AT SECONDCHANCE.ORG/MYFREEWAY

OPTION #2: WATCH THE DVD

PURCHASE THE GROUP DISCUSSION DVD
AT SECONDCHANCE.ORG/STORE

SUPPLIES YOU WILL NEED

- [ ] PEN OR PENCIL
- [ ] OPEN HEART
- [ ] GLUE
- [ ] YELLOW STICKY NOTES
- [ ] TRUCKLOAD OF COURAGE
- [ ] WHITE STRING
- [ ] SCISSORS
- [ ] PRE-FILLED HELIUM BALLOONS
- [ ] BIBLE
- [ ] THIS WORKBOOK (OF COURSE!!!)

HERE IS THE WORLD. BEAUTIFUL AND TERRIBLE

THINGS WILL HAPPEN. DON'T BE AFRAID.

FREDERICK BUECHNER

FREEWAY

FREEWAY

THE STORY OF FRIENDS

Freeway started like most good things: with a few friends and simple stories. It began with lives dipped in struggle, beauty, and the search to find grace. The foundations were laid over pasta with J.R. and Diane, family swim parties with Kevin and Robin, and San Diego Charger games with my best friend, Jud. It was birthed from conversations around crackling fire pits in the spring, summer talks at the Carlsbad Seawall, and plainspoken confessions over raisin bagels in the fall.

Each of us shared about both the joy and the ache that life brings. It's never just one or the other. Life deals in both smiles and salty tears—and sometimes more sorrow than we would like.

As friends often do, we asked earnest questions like, "How are you? How is your heart? You doing OK?" And in those basic questions, we patiently waited until the truth slowly bubbled out through the tiny cracks of our well-crafted facades.

Though this probably won't surprise you, we lied to one another at first. Of course, like any soul protecting secrets, we shared watered-down life updates and threw in a couple of cryptic sidetracks for good measure. But if we waited long enough and fought the temptation to revert back to trivial topics, something more authentic would emerge—the struggle of life, the doubt in who we were, and our fears.

I shared first. In the summer, I confessed that I had been verbally cutting my teenage son down. I had become skilled at whacking him with nit-picking criticisms about his oily, uncombed hair and the careless way he mowed my precious lawn.

Sadly, my heavy-handed commentary was sucking out my son's confidence and left him low. I was worried about the kind of father I was becoming. My son was living with a bully, not a loving father. It was hard to say that, and now even hard to write, but it was true.

Later in the summer I told a close friend about the negative tongue-lashings going off in my head. It was like a mental whipping of internal indictments that continually questioned my worth. The words were my own cat-o'-nine-tails knotted up with phrases like "stupid idiot" but with a lot more gangsta in it. I believed I was a fraud just like those fast-talking hawkers on late-night infomercials. I so disliked who I was that one night in a hotel room in Atlanta, I sucker punched myself in the face in utter frustration. My mind was sizzling with shame.

So that was my stuff. Though it was really difficult to admit those things to my friends, I'm glad I shared everything I was struggling with. And I'm glad my friends really loved me through it and still wanted me in their lives.

Then it was their turn to share. I gladly listened to their stories. They told me about how spiritually, emotionally, and physically hollow they felt. In rambling sentences, they shared how life was feeling really heavy.

We talked about psychotic family episodes and that not-so-sunny job market. They shared how it hurt that so-and-so had unfriended them on Facebook and how they were insanely jealous of their next-door neighbor's perfect little family. Not to mention that obnoxious "My Kid Was Student of the Month" sticker slapped on Miss Perfect's brand-new Lexus 350.

They told stories of mental illness and the guilt of having to put the broken-down bodies of elderly parents into hospice. There were breast-cancer scares, pets that ran away, and one friend who was trying to figure out how he was going to pay for another brain surgery for his kid who was suffering from seizures.

This was our life, and it felt like it was more sourdough than cupcake. All of us were doing our part as best as we could, but we still felt like we were baking a story that was becoming more cynical, with sprinkles of insecurity and a dash of hopelessness.

But even in the midst of our manic states of craziness, brain surgeries, and Facebook unfriending, we believed we could be better. And I don't mean better looking or a better person or a better Christian, but more well inside. We hoped that amazing grace was more than just a Sunday-morning hymn and that Jesus could love us like he loved all those busted-up souls back in his town.

We grasped tightly to our tiny faith and believed our fractured hearts could eventually be patched up. Or if we got lucky, maybe Jesus would give us a new heart altogether. That would be really nice. And though none of us were exactly free like we wanted to be, we truly hoped that there might be a possibility of it happening one day.

The truth is, all of us are more human, more wobbly, and more fragile than we wish we actually were. But we are also more holy, more heavenly, and stronger than we could ever imagine. And this is what we will cling to in the days ahead. For every heart cracked open, every story looking for redemption, and every person longing to live the free way, this is for you. So let's begin.

WHAT DO YOU AND YOUR FRIENDS TALK ABOUT?

CHECK THE MOST TALKED ABOUT TOPICS.

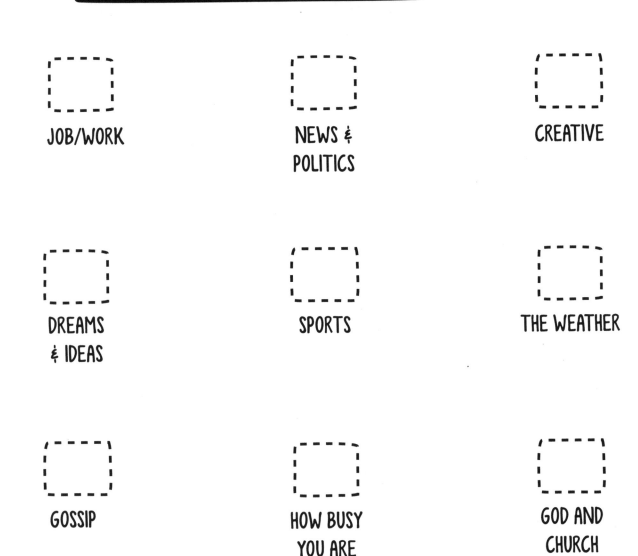

☐ JOB/WORK

☐ NEWS & POLITICS

☐ CREATIVE

☐ DREAMS & IDEAS

☐ SPORTS

☐ THE WEATHER

☐ GOSSIP

☐ HOW BUSY YOU ARE

☐ GOD AND CHURCH STUFF

☐ MOVIES &
TV SHOWS

☐ OTHER
PEOPLE'S
DRAMA

☐ HURTS &
STRUGGLES

☐ FAMILY
& KIDS

☐ LOVE LIFE

☐ SCHOOL

☐ HOT TOPICS

☐ OTHER:

WHAT WOULD YOU PREFER TO TALK WITH THEM ABOUT?

- -

- -

BE ANXIOUS FOR NOTHING, BUT IN EVERYTHING BY

PRAYER AND SUPPLICATION WITH THANKSGIVING LET

YOUR REQUESTS BE MADE KNOWN TO GOD.

AND THE PEACE OF GOD, WHICH SURPASSES ALL

COMPREHENSION, WILL GUARD YOUR HEARTS AND

YOUR MINDS IN CHRIST JESUS.

PHILIPPIANS 4:6-7

FREEWAY

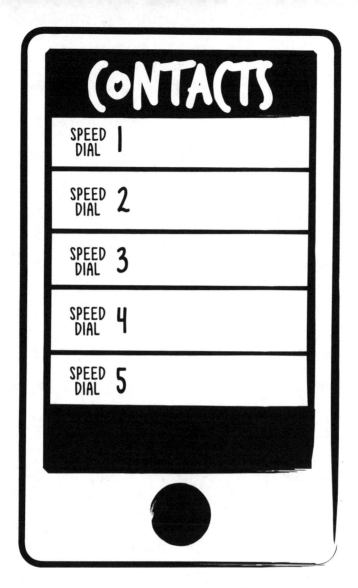

WHO DO YOU TALK TO WHEN YOU'RE HURTING OR WHEN LIFE IS TOUGH?

WRITE THEIR NAMES ON THE SPEED DIAL LINES.

INTRO

A PROD
PARTY

ICALS

SHARING STORIES AND ENJOYING THE COMPANY OF FRIENDS IS ALWAYS A WONDERFUL PLACE TO BEGIN.

PREPARE

A SHORT INTRODUCTION TO A BIG IDEA.

INTRO
A PRODIGAL'S PARTY

Life is a weird but wonderful mystery that none of us can fully understand. We just believe that we're meant to show up each morning, throw on a pot of coffee, hurry out the door, try our best to survive, and accept that both good and suffering will equally share the stage of our frail and beautiful stories.

There are good parts—having birthday parties, running faster in new shoes, being debt free, going to springtime weddings, and smelling the sweetness of newborn babies. These are everyday gifts for us to savor and enjoy.

Then there are really hard parts—our battles with loneliness, the fight with our muffin top, kids who need chemo again, that affair and the divorce, our silent suffering, and our unseen addictions. These are the parts we want to begin to talk about.

For it is the dings, the skinned knees, and the broken bones of life that Jesus is most interested in. Whether we like it or not, pain is part of life, and our divine rescuer doesn't bring a small box of Band-Aids or a couple of Advil. He brings supernatural healing, and if you and I are being honest, healing is exactly what we need right now.

We hustle to be noticed and long to be accepted as we are. We've become what everyone else wants us to be—yet the best gift we could bring the world is being people God created us to be. As writer Henri Nouwen once said, "One of the tragedies of our life is that we keep forgetting who we are."

Too many of us believe the lie that we need to sanitize our scandals, brush away our grief, and cover up our scars. We're frightened that our fumbling, stumbling mess of hypocrisy and shame will soon be exposed.

Like a birthday-party magician protecting all of his tricks, we worry that someone might catch us screaming at our kids before church or snicker at our sexual history or discover that we take Prozac. We hold tight to the secrets that we sneak Hershey bars into movie theaters, lied about our SAT scores, and love eating those shiny hot dogs from the local gas station.

We're scared that if the world sees how messy our lives really are, they won't like us one bit. They'll leave us out of the cool kids party and our invitation will surprisingly get lost in the mail. So we bury all of our hurts and struggles underneath lies of perfection. We pretend to be OK when really we're not. And then we eventually go nuts and become so fed up that we start throwing things at our poor dog ... or worse.

Maybe all that stellar advice from our parents, the religious know-it-alls, and the self-esteem gurus fell flat. It helped our skinned knees a little, but it didn't bring healing for our broken heart.

This moment is an invitation (or maybe an intervention) to experience a new freedom. It is not the *Braveheart* or Declaration of Independence kind of freedom, but the kind of freedom that can shake souls to the core. I'm talking about the type of liberation that can break through the facade of having to fake like we're OK all the time.

God wants to make a deal with us. If we hand over our insecurities, let go of moralistic religion, and bravely admit our secrets, he will heal our hearts and give each of us a new life.

Our gracious Father will not add conditions to his love for us. He doesn't ask us to first clean up our sloppy messes. He does not approach us with a guarded politeness or condescendingly pat us on the head and squeeze our dirty cheeks. He simply invites us to jump into Daddy's arms and let him be our source of love and identity. He beckons us to live the free way.

And if right now, we sat together at a Starbucks and you told me your story—

> how you're scared that you're not enough,
> and that you feel like a screw up,
> and how you lie about this and that,
> or how you wish your friends would invite you over more often

—I would hold your hand in a non-weird sorta way, look you straight in the eye, and tell you this:

You are loved more than you could possibly know, and everything is going to be OK.

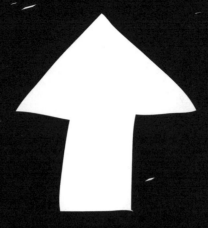

TRUST IN THE LORD WITH ALL YOUR HEART.

LEAN NOT ON YOUR OWN UNDERSTANDING.

IN ALL YOUR WAYS SUBMIT TO HIM, AND HE WILL MAKE

YOUR PATHS STRAIGHT.

PROVERBS 3:5-6 NIV

FREEWAY

While reading the stories in the Bible, I learned that God's favorites are know-it-all prodigals, runaway sheep, used-up whores, and cunning thieves and liars. People just like you and me.

We can rest in the truth that we have a Father who hears our feeble prayers and knows that we are fickle and flawed. His eyes are filled with kindness even when we spill the Cheerios and burn the toast and blame the kids for it all. He wipes away tears of regret and hands out grace-filled snow cones on hot judgmental days. Jesus is for us, and he really wants to help.

So this is your invitation to stop running and to RSVP for the celebration. Whoever you are, whatever you've done, wherever you've been, and whatever your story may be, you can always come home. Grace awaits, and your Father welcomes you to a prodigal's party. Come inside ... we have all been waiting for you.

EXPLORE

EXERCISES TO HELP YOU EXPLORE YOUR STORY.

STICK A PHOTO HERE!

GLUE A PICTURE THAT REPRESENTS A MEANINGFUL PART OF YOUR STORY.
JOT DOWN WHY THIS PICTURE MEANS SOMETHING TO YOU.

---

*BTW, BE READY TO SHARE ABOUT THIS PICTURE WITH YOUR GROUP.

IN WHAT AREAS OF YOUR LIFE DO YOU FEEL KINDA STUCK?

STUCK IN THE PAST? STUCK IN PAIN? STUCK IN BAD HABITS? WRITE SOME OF YOUR THOUGHTS HERE.

WHATEVER YOU'RE READY FOR IS READY FOR YOU.

FREEWAY

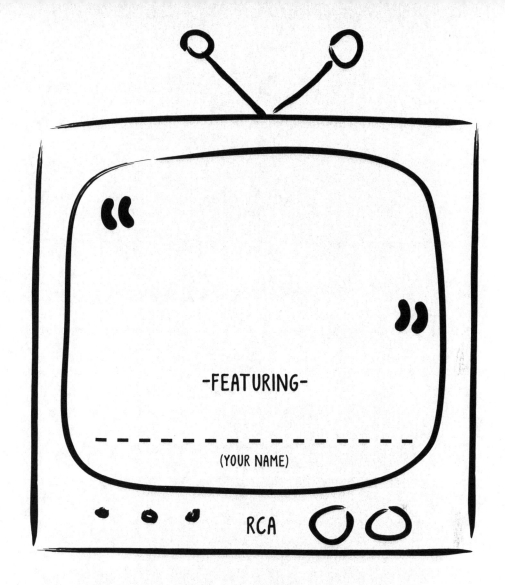

" "

-FEATURING-

― ― ― ― ― ― ― ― ― ― ― ―
(YOUR NAME)

RCA

IF YOUR LIFE WAS A REALITY TV SHOW, WHAT WOULD YOU CALL IT?

WRITE IT ON THE TV SCREEN. BE CREATIVE!

SHARE

MEET WITH YOUR FRIENDS AND GO THROUGH THE
GROUP QUESTIONS TOGETHER.

GROUP QUESTIONS
INTRO: A PRODIGAL'S PARTY

Just as I have loved you, you should love each other.
Your love for one another will prove to the world that you are my disciples.
John 13:34-35

This first group session is all about getting together and preparing for the *Freeway* process. It is designed to allow everyone to get to know each other and set the stage for the coming weeks. Roll out some cheesecake or mixed nuts or do a barbecue or go out to dinner. Just enjoy one another, share stories, and do these group exercises together.

PLAY THE DVD OR STREAM THE VIDEO ONLINE AT SECONDCHANCE.ORG/MYFREEWAY

1. Have everyone share about themselves for a few minutes. Use the photos you glued onto page 31 as a starting point.

2. Why are you interested in going through *Freeway*? What are your hopes for the coming weeks?

3. Go over the —Group Promise—page together. See page 38. Make sure everyone understands the commitment. Sign and date it.

4. Put on your "Freedom Strings," and then take a group photo together.

GROUP PROMISE

I, [_____], COMMIT TO THESE BASIC FREEWAY GROUP PROMISES. THIS IS MY ALL-IN PLEDGE SHOWING MY COMMITMENT TO FREEDOM IN MY OWN LIFE AND FOR MY GROUP MEMBERS.

- [ ] I WILL BE ON TIME, COME PREPARED AND SHOW UP WITH MY WHOLE HEART.

- [ ] THIS IS 1000 PERCENT CONFIDENTIAL. EVERYTHING SHARED IN THE GROUP STAYS IN THE GROUP.

- [ ] I WILL RESPECT OTHER GROUP MEMBERS BY NOT GOBBLING UP ALL THE TALK TIME.

- [ ] I WILL NOT TRY TO FIX PEOPLE, PREACH A SERMON, OR GIVE UNSOLICITED ADVICE.

- [ ] WHEN I SHARE IN THE GROUP I WILL SHARE PRIMARILY ABOUT MYSELF AND NOT ABOUT OTHERS.

- [ ] I WILL TRUST GOD TO DO THE WORK IN ALL OF US.

[_____]

SIGN YOUR NAME HERE

[_____]   [_____]

DATE   LOCATION

FREEDOM STRINGS

AS A SYMBOL OF YOUR PROMISE TO ONE ANOTHER AND TO GOD, EVERYONE IS ASKED TO WEAR A SIMPLE WHITE STRING WHILE GOING THROUGH FREEWAY. LET THIS STRING BE A REMINDER OF YOUR COMMITMENT TO PURSUING FREEDOM.

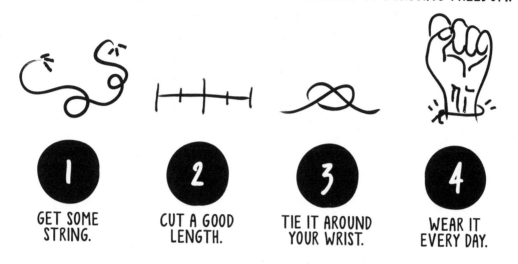

1 GET SOME STRING.

2 CUT A GOOD LENGTH.

3 TIE IT AROUND YOUR WRIST.

4 WEAR IT EVERY DAY.

GROUP CONTACT INFORMATION

NAME   PHONE   EMAIL

SNAP A GROUP PHOTO AND POST IT !!

EXPRESS YOUR PERSONALITY
AND SAY "CHEESE!"

TWITTER   INSTAGRAM   FACEBOOK

#MYFREEWAY

JUMP IN

LET'S TRY SOME STUFF THIS WEEK!

PRAY SIMPLE PRAYERS

When you're in the car this week, spend a little time praying some simple prayers. Nothing fancy or long-winded. Pray for an open heart. Pray for your group members by name. Invite God into everything. This should be pretty easy, right?

MY FAVORITE VERSES

This week, type up your favorite Bible verses and print them out on a piece of paper. Stick them around your house, in your office, or in your car. See how many of these verses you can memorize in a week.

CREATE YOUR "MY FREEWAY" ACCOUNT AT
SECONDCHANCE.ORG/MYFREEWAY
FOR DAILY DEVOTIONS, DOWNLOADS & VIDEOS

REMEMBER

JOURNAL, SCRIBBLE, & DOODLE YOUR THOUGHTS.

LIFE IS A GORGEOUS, BROKEN GIFT. SIX BILLION PIECES WAITING TO BE FIXED.

-SLEEPING AT LAST-

FREEWAY

STEP 1

AWAR

ENESS

A SIMPLE INVITATION TO SLOW DOWN, LET BLURRY EYES
SEE, AND LET A LOVING GOD QUIETLY SPEAK TO US.

PREPARE

A SHORT INTRODUCTION TO A BIG IDEA.

STEP 1
AWARENESS

It is a classic Hollywood scene: a voice shouts at four frightened souls in possession of a witch's broomstick. Emerald cauldrons spew flames and smoke into the sky. "Come back tomorrow ... you ungrateful creatures," the Great Wizard yells as his bulbous head floats over a pit of fire.

Then, in the scene's climactic moment, a mangy little dog pulls back the green drape to reveal a worn-out circus magician cranking levers and pushing buttons.

"Pay no attention to that man behind the curtain," the wizard commands them. But the hocus-pocus is over, the illusion is gone, and it's time for a frightened girl from Kansas and even the Great Wizard himself to see way beyond the rainbow.

Our freedom surprisingly starts with becoming more aware of the great cover-up. It begins when we accept that all of us have veiled habits, blind spots, and hidden places in our hearts. And whatever the issues might be, we must instigate our very own Wizard of Oz moment that pulls back the curtain on the mischief maker. If we want to be free, we must be aware of the troublemaking con man behind the scenes.

But many of us will only take action against the great and powerful Oz when we can see what he is doing to us, which is of course the tricky part. We can't see how pain, loss, and unforgiveness pull levers; send us on meaningless witch hunts; and trap us in haunted forests.

Unresolved pain keeps us in a dead life where we are stripped of anything authentic. We protect ourselves with detached ambivalence to guarantee we never get hurt again. Our sadness is masked in seething anger, and our daily lives become grinding, shallow, and less than magical. We gut it out and hope one day it might get better.

Some try to fix their hurts by replacing pain with short-term pleasure. Compulsive behaviors like alcohol addiction, self injury, online fixations, illicit affairs, unrestrained shopping sprees, and the aptly named "comfort food" all keep us numbed up and "happy." Pain has us completely owned.

And though we might not understand what's going on, thankfully Jesus does— and he is going to deal with it all. He promises us it doesn't have to be this way.

Jesus was there when our dad left our mom for another woman and understands why we give our hearts to strangers in bars who tell us we're pretty. Jesus cried with us when the coach humiliated us on the practice field, and he knows what it felt like when we were the last one picked for the kickball team.

Jesus gets why we drown our sorrows in three bottles of cheap Merlot and why we eat elephantine amounts of Rocky Road ice cream when we're lonely.

As the psalmist sang, "If I go up to the heavens, you are there; if I make my bed in the depths, you are there" (Ps. 139:8 NLT). And he says that everything you've gone through, everything you perceived to be lost, everything that has been broken has not gone unnoticed. He has been there, and he wants to do something about it.

Sure, the hyper-religious will gloss over our troubled hearts with snappy Bible verses and cheesy prayers and will shame us by hinting we're the defective ones. Or we become our own cotton-candy cliché peddlers by convincing ourselves that our hurts are "not a big deal" or that we should just "look on the bright side."

Oh, and let's not forget the testosterone-guzzling, boot-strapping MMA types who tell us to "just suck it up and quit your crying. Arrrgh!" I don't say that to judge but to simply point out that they might be as blind to what is going on as we are. The man behind the curtain is also fooling them.

Right now we can become aware of what God wants to show us by embracing our great liberator, Jesus. He is the divine emancipator and a celestial warrior-poet hell-bent on giving creation a second chance at freedom. He is not some ancient religious deity, motivational nugget hawker, or longhaired hippie dressed in a white terry-cloth bathrobe. Rather, Jesus is the compassionate truth bearer who shines on our suffering. With his glory he reveals the hidden nooks and crannies of our fears. And now all we must do is rally the same courage of that little mangy dog and bite into the curtain … and pull.

Awareness begins with accepting the simple gift of slowness. The Trappist monk Thomas Merton once said, "Hurry ruins saints," and writer Eugene

HUMAN BEINGS ARE POOR SELF-EXAMINERS,

SUBJECT TO SUPERSTITION, BIAS,

PREJUDICE, AND A PROFOUND TENDENCY

TO SEE WHAT THEY WANT TO SEE RATHER

THAN WHAT IS REALLY THERE.

M. SCOTT PECK

FREEWAY

Peterson plainly stated that "busyness is the enemy of spirituality." What most of us might not realize is that our hustle-and-bustle lives are the drapes that hang over our hearts.

Our typical days involve sifting through a plague of 4,327 unread emails, counting calories in Venti Frappuccinos, reading Twitter streams, doing buckets of laundry, and shoving the kids off to Tae Kwon Do practice. Distraction and busyness are the sicknesses of our generation and the cause of our blindness. Our lives are loaded up with so much momentum, energy, and blaring noise. Slowing down will take some real focus and intentionality.

Jesus now invites us into restful moments and his quiet mercies. Our great liberator does not shout or speak to us through a green floating head. He is the God of Elijah, who gently speaks. He wasn't in the earthquake or in wind or in the fire. He was in the still, small voice. And in this moment, he speaks to you of your emerging freedom. He says, "Come, my beloved. Open your eyes. Awaken your heart. Pull back the veil. Your freedom is here."

EXPLORE

EXERCISES TO HELP YOU EXPLORE YOUR STORY.

IN YOUR LIFE, WHAT ARE SOME POSSIBLE HIDDEN BUTTONS BEING PUSHED?

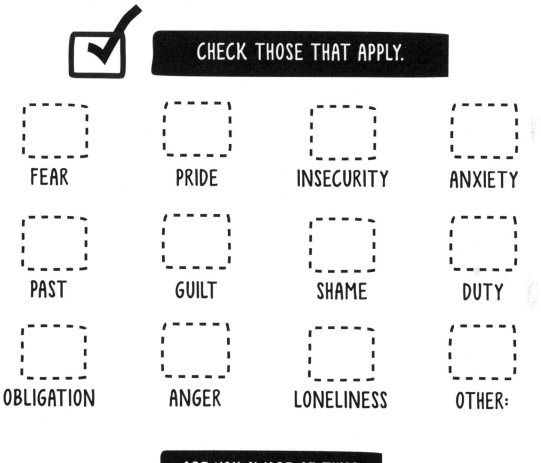

CHECK THOSE THAT APPLY.

☐ FEAR

☐ PRIDE

☐ INSECURITY

☐ ANXIETY

☐ PAST

☐ GUILT

☐ SHAME

☐ DUTY

☐ OBLIGATION

☐ ANGER

☐ LONELINESS

☐ OTHER:

ARE YOU AWARE OF THIS?

WHAT IS CAUSING YOU WORRY OR CONCERN RIGHT NOW?

LIST THE TOP THREE:

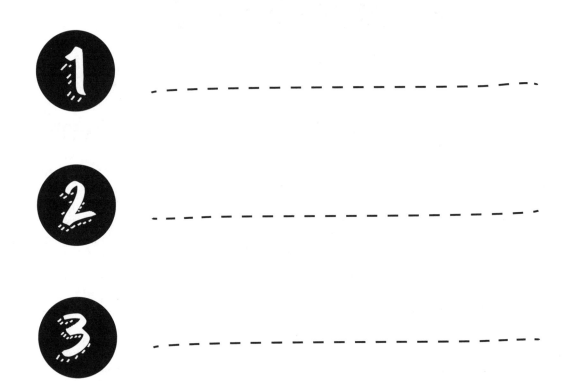

1 -

2 -

3 -

ARE YOU SLEEPING WITH YOUR SMARTPHONE?

CHECK THE BOX THAT BEST APPLIES TO YOU.

☐ IT IS SURGICALLY ATTACHED

☐ YES!

☐ PERHAPS, BUT I'M NOT SAYING

☐ NOT ALL THE TIME

☐ NO, JUST MY PILLOW

☐ NEXT QUESTION, PLEASE

TAKE A WILD GUESS HOW MANY TIMES YOU MIGHT CHECK YOUR PHONE ON A TYPICAL DAY. ☐

MY BIG OLE DISTRACTIONS LIST

CIRCLE YOUR TOP THREE DAILY DISTRACTIONS.

TV

SOCIAL MEDIA

EMAIL

CRAZY
SCHEDULE

PHONE
CALLS

WORK

BUSY
THOUGHTS

ANGRY BIRDS/
WORDS WITH
FRIENDS

SURFING
THE NET

SPORTS / GYM

HEALTH
ISSUES

PARTYING

TEXTING

KIDS' STUFF

LOVE LIFE

RELATIONSHIPS &
FRIENDSHIPS

RESPONSIBILITIES
AT HOME/
FAMILY

HOW FAST IS YOUR LIFE RIGHT NOW?

 CHECK THOSE THAT APPLY.

RESTING

LIMPING

WALKING

RUNNING

RACING

SUPERSONIC

HOW LONG HAS IT BEEN THIS WAY?

DAYS? WEEKS? MONTHS?

??? EXPLAIN WHY YOU CHECKED THAT BOX

IF YOU DON'T LIKE HOW FAST YOU'RE GOING, CAN YOU CHANGE IT?

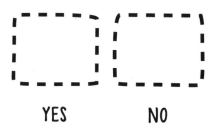

YES   NO

IF YOUR ANSWER IS YES WHAT COULD YOU DO RIGHT NOW?

I COULD CHANGE...

HOW WELL ARE YOU HEARING GOD?

MARK AN X ON THE LINE

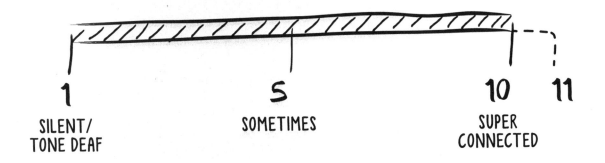

1
SILENT/
TONE DEAF

5
SOMETIMES

10
SUPER
CONNECTED

11

HOW AVAILABLE ARE YOU?

MARK AN X ON THE LINE

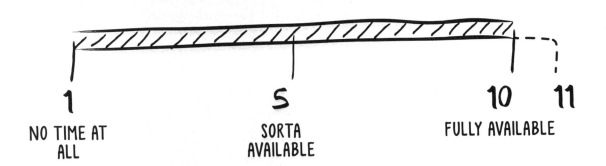

1
NO TIME AT
ALL

5
SORTA
AVAILABLE

10
FULLY AVAILABLE

11

HOW HARD IS IT TO BE STILL?

MARK AN X ON THE LINE

IMPOSSIBLE
RIGHT NOW

TAKES SOME
EFFORT

SUPER EASY

HOW NOISY IS YOUR LIFE?

MARK AN X ON THE LINE

DECIBELS

0   10   30   50   80   90   100   110   120

NOISE OF
BREATHING

CITY
TRAFFIC

CHAIN
SAW

JET
TAKING
OFF

WHAT STRESSES YOU OUT?

1.

2.

3.

4.

5.

PEOPLE ?

SITUATIONS ?

MONEY ?

FAMILY ?

WORK ?

OTHER ?

WHAT HAPPENS WHEN YOU ARE STRESSED ?

1.

2.

3.

4.

5.

HOW CAN YOU RELIEVE STRESS IN A POSITIVE WAY ? + + + + + + +

↑ ↑ ↑ ↑ ↑ ↑ ↑ ↑

HOW WELL DO YOU HANDLE STRESS ?

HOW STRESSED ARE YOU?

1 - - 2 - - 3 - - 4 - - 5

LOW
STRESS

HIGH
STRESS

IN THE *WIZARD OF OZ*, A MANGY LITTLE DOG SIMPLY

WALKED UP TO THE CURTAIN AND YANKED IT BACK.

WHAT COULD YOUR WIZARD OF OZ MOMENT LOOK LIKE

THAT WOULD MOVE YOU CLOSER TO FREEDOM?

FREEWAY

OK, LET'S JUST ASSUME WE ALL HAVE BLIND SPOTS. TAKE A WILD GUESS WHAT YOURS MIGHT BE.

- -

- -

- -

- -

- -

- -

- -

- -

INSTEAD OF REGRETTING WHERE YOU'VE BEEN, GIVE THANKS FOR WHERE YOU'RE GOING.

FREEWAY

WHAT AM I LEARNING ABOUT MYSELF?

ABOUT GOD?

ARE YOU READY TO SHARE WHAT YOU'RE LEARNING WITH SOMEONE?

[ ] ABSOLUTELY!

[ ] I'M REALLY NERVOUS ABOUT SHARING ... BUT I WILL.

[ ] NOT YET, BUT SOON.

[ ] NO WAY.

FROM YOUR HEART, WRITE A ONE-LINE PRAYER TO GOD.

SHARE

MEET WITH YOUR FRIENDS AND GO THROUGH THE
GROUP QUESTIONS TOGETHER.

GROUP QUESTIONS
STEP I: AWARENESS

Search me, God, and know my heart; test me
and know my anxious thoughts.

Psalm 139:23 NIV

1. Take some time to discuss the pre-work: what you filled out, what you think, how you feel about it, and what changes—if any—you'd like to make in your life as you move toward freedom. What did you learn about yourself by doing the reading and exercises this week?

PLAY THE DVD OR STREAM THE VIDEO ONLINE AT
SECONDCHANCE.ORG/MYFREEWAY

2. What does it mean to you to be "self aware"? How would our lives be different if we were more self-aware? Does God think it is important to be aware? Why?

3. Why do you think it can be so hard to get in touch with what's going on inside of us? What keeps us from growing in self-awareness?

4. What is the opposite of "self-aware"? When have you seen it hurt someone? How has it hurt you in the past?

5. Have you ever thought something was good for you and then you discovered that it wasn't? Maybe it was a habit (like checking emails first thing in the morning) or a relationship (with that abusive someone).

6. How distracted are you in your life? How fast are you running? Is it possible you're running from something?

OPTIONAL GROUP ACTIVITY

Have someone in your group close his or her eyes and describe something in the room. See how much detail that person can come up with and how accurate he or she is. Take turns trying this experiment.

JUMP IN

LET'S TRY SOME STUFF THIS WEEK!

CAPTURE SOME ALONE TIME

Pick out a favorite spot that is quiet and undisturbed. Spend some time alone with God. Fifteen, thirty or sixty minutes? You choose. During this time, do whatever helps you listen to God.

DISRUPT YOUR DIGITAL ROUTINE

Think about your typical routine with your phone, social media, email and any other piece of technology. Figure out some strategies to silence them or have them be less intrusive. When tempted to fill quietness with a digital distraction, try enjoying the stillness. See what happens.

WATCH A SUNRISE OR A SUNSET

What is it about the brilliant clash of light and dark that inspires and awakens beauty at the beginning and end of each day? Share the picture, explain how this moment impacts you in your own awareness.

CREATE YOUR "MY FREEWAY" ACCOUNT AT
SECONDCHANCE.ORG/MYFREEWAY
FOR DAILY DEVOTIONS, DOWNLOADS & VIDEOS

REMEMBER

JOURNAL, SCRIBBLE, & DOODLE YOUR THOUGHTS.

DOODLE HERE

KEEP YOUR HEART WILD AND FREE.

FREEWAY

STEP 2

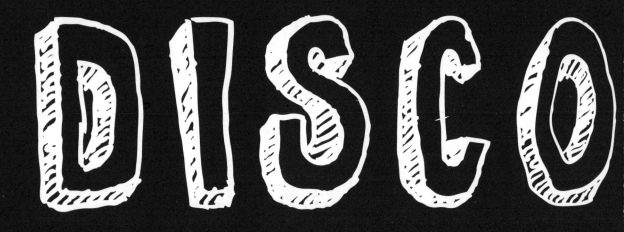

DISCO

VERY

EXPLORING OUR STORY OF STRUGGLE WITH
COMPASSIONATE CURIOSITY.

PREPARE

A SHORT INTRODUCTION TO A BIG IDEA.

STEP 2
DISCOVERY

On November 26, 2011, NASA launched the Atlas V 541 rocket from Cape Canaveral, Florida. Joining the *Atlas* for the 350,000,000-mile journey into space was the Curiosity Rover. Its mission was to investigate the possibilities of life on the red planet Mars.

Outfitted with the standard scientific gear, the rover also carried 1.2 million inscribed names on it, including those of the president of the United States, senior space officials, and earthlings from around the globe who submitted their names through the NASA website.

But one lucky Midwest schoolgirl had the opportunity to sign her name on the actual spacecraft. Twelve-year-old Clara Ma had won NASA's essay competition, which allowed her to name the Mars rover *Curiosity*. She wrote in her winning essay, "Curiosity is the passion that drives us through our everyday lives."

Clara knew that the one who placed the stars in the sky has planted in every human the wonder of exploration. As kids we loved discovering the world in all its delicious possibilities. We had the thrill of squishing earthworms in our hands, trying out foot-massage chairs at carnivals, and building our own cardboard spaceships whose mission was the moon. God placed imagination, what-ifs, and whimsy deep within our hearts. He must have known that discovery is how real change happens.

The heaven maker now invites us to uncover far-off places in our stories and find new life on the planet called You. We can bravely touch the scary things of our stories without protective gloves on. You and I can feel the fullness of all of our history and bravely stand in our truth.

Jesus says that we don't have to be afraid of who we really are. In order to be free, we must run toward the pain, not away from it. As philosopher Søren Kierkegaard wrote, "To dare is to lose one's footing momentarily. Not to dare is to lose oneself." If we can't face our fears, then we can't really change.

True spiritual growth means asking the tough questions and going forward into the darkness, armed with a dozen flashlights of truth. It is a beautifully poetic process that awakens hidden passions, fears, and other artifacts in the deep space of our souls.

The spiritual quest, the quest for true healing, always starts with honest questions. It is filled with wondrous curiosity and asks:

Who am I really?
What are my weaknesses?
Who tells me who I am?
What nagging fears do I constantly carry around?
What do I dwell on?
How authentic am I?
How receptive am I to change?

This is the launchpad into freedom's heavenly places.

So as we start to poke around in our stories for what's been hiding, I suggest that you do it with a big dose of "compassionate curiosity." Be gentle and kind with yourself. This is not a witch hunt or the Spanish Inquisition. It's not a jury trial or a beauty competition to see who has the best scars to showcase. The mission is to find and document what God wants you to discover. That's all.

It is also important to note that the Curiosity Rover didn't travel to the red planet alone. It needed the Atlas V 541 rocket to get there. As we go forward, discovering the parts of our hearts that hurt, we should do it with a friend. Our friends will help us uncover our strengths and weaknesses. But don't let them try to fix you; just let them help you get there, because Jesus is the only fixer and freedom giver.

But the enemy of soul exploration sends lightening storms, thick fog, and technical difficulties of confusion to keep you going nowhere fast. He fights against you exploring the roots of your suffering because you might discover Jesus's earth-shaking grace. He knows that if he can kidnap your heart, he can kidnap your hope. God says, "Let's grow," but the enemy says, "Not today."

Freedom comes through discovering the pain, living authentically with it, and letting Jesus drown it in heaven's grace. You don't have to be afraid to look or even pretend it's not there. Twelve-year-old Clara Ma and her award-winning essay were right all along: curiosity is what makes us human, and discovery is a divine exploration.

EXPLORE

EXERCISES TO HELP YOU EXPLORE YOUR STORY.

WHAT FEELS BROKEN?

CHECK THE BOX OR BOXES THAT APPLY. EXPLAIN BELOW.

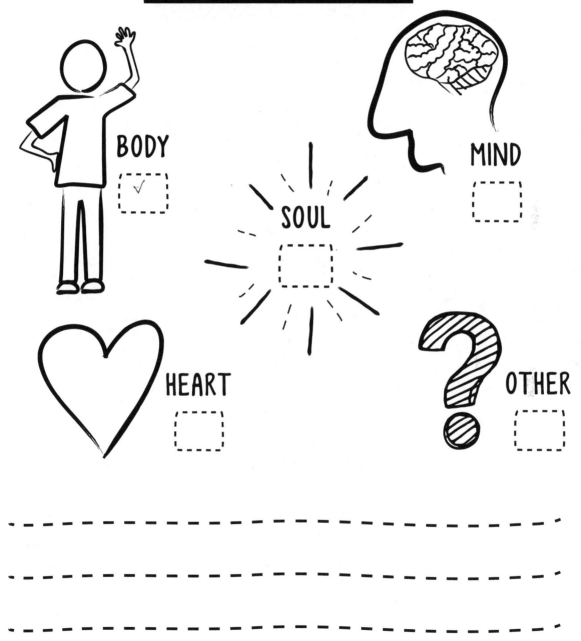

BODY ✓

MIND ☐

SOUL ☐

HEART ☐

OTHER ☐

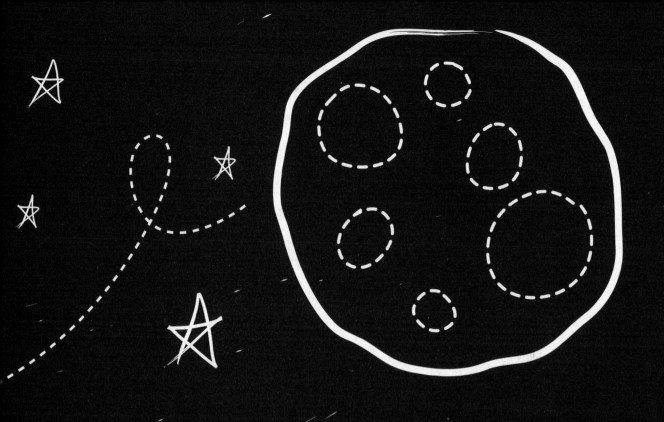

WHAT DO YOU NEED TO EXPLORE?

WHO CAN HELP YOU ON THIS MISSION?

SOUL SCAVENGER HUNT

CHECK THE BOX FOR EACH
QUESTION. BE HONEST.

START

ARE YOU WORRIED
OR SCARED ABOUT
ANYTHING?

YES NO

NOW DO THIS AGAIN,
BUT TRY TO BE EVEN
MORE HONEST.

HOW ARE YOUR
RELATIONSHIPS?

GOOD NOT GOOD

ARE YOU A
PEOPLE PLEASER?

YES NO

ARE YOU SLEEPING WELL?

YES NO

DO YOU LIKE WHO
YOU ARE?

YES NO

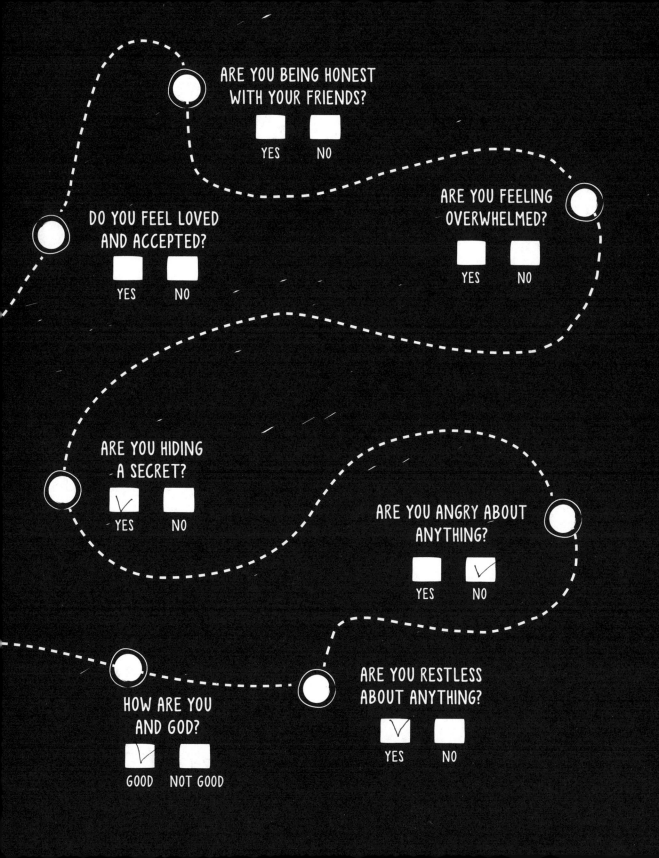

WRITE THE YEAR YOU WERE THE HAPPIEST!

AND THE HARDEST YEAR?

WHY WAS IT THE HAPPIEST YEAR? DESCRIBE IT.

WHY WAS IT THE HARDEST YEAR? DESCRIBE IT.

LIST THE THINGS THAT SCARE YOU THAT YOU'RE OK WITH TELLING PEOPLE.

SPIDERS? THE DARK? HEIGHTS?

SCARY THINGS

FEAR INC.

LIST THE THINGS THAT SCARE YOU THAT YOU DON'T WANT OTHERS TO KNOW.

BEING ALONE? A SECRET? ADDICTION? INTIMACY?

GOD
IS LOVE.
PERFECT
LOVE
CASTS OUT
ALL FEAR.

- 1 JOHN 4:18 -

FREEWAY

THE SCARY MONSTER INSIDE

WE ALL HAVE THINGS INSIDE OF US THAT WE DON'T WANT TO FACE.

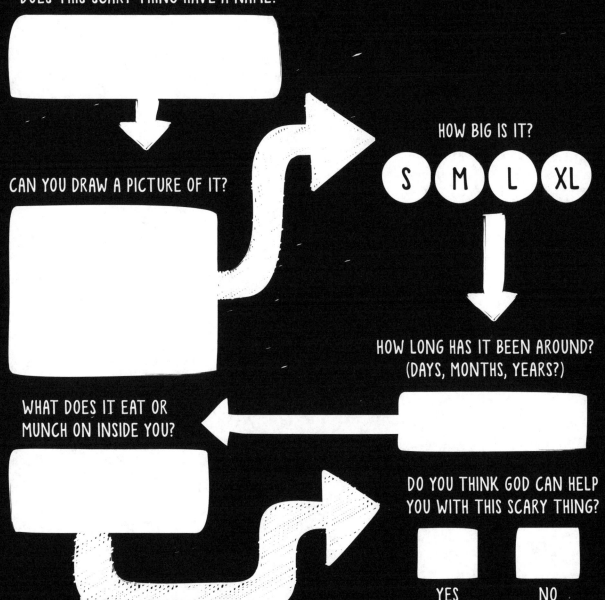

DOES THIS SCARY THING HAVE A NAME?

CAN YOU DRAW A PICTURE OF IT?

HOW BIG IS IT?

S M L XL

HOW LONG HAS IT BEEN AROUND?
(DAYS, MONTHS, YEARS?)

WHAT DOES IT EAT OR
MUNCH ON INSIDE YOU?

DO YOU THINK GOD CAN HELP
YOU WITH THIS SCARY THING?

YES   NO

WHAT ARE YOUR TOP 3 STRENGTHS?

STEP 1: CHECKMARK THE 7 STRENGTHS THAT ARE MOST LIKE YOU.

STEP 2: FROM THE 7 STRENGTHS THAT YOU CHECKED, WRITE DOWN THE TOP 3 THAT ARE MOST LIKE YOU.

ADAPTABLE
I ADJUST READILY TO NEW OR MODIFIED CONDITIONS.

AMBITIOUS
I AM DETERMINED TO SUCCEED AND GET AHEAD.

ANALYTICAL
I DISSECT AND DIGEST WHATEVER IS GOING ON.

CARING
I CONCERN MYSELF WITH THE WELL-BEING OF OTHERS.

CAUTIOUS
I AM CAREFUL TO MAKE SURE OF WHAT IS GOING ON.

COMPETITIVE
I STRIVE TO WIN AGAINST OTHERS.

DEVOTED
I AM DEDICATED TO SOME PEOPLE, ACTIVITIES, OR PURPOSES.

FAIR
I ACT JUSTLY, EQUITABLY, AND IMPARTIALLY.

FLEXIBLE
I ACT IN THE APPROPRIATE MANNER FOR THE MOMENT.

FORCEFUL
I ACT WITH CONVICTION, POWER, AND DRIVE.

HELPFUL
I GIVE ASSISTANCE TO OTHERS WHO ARE IN NEED.

INCLUSIVE
I BRING PEOPLE TOGETHER IN ORDER TO REACH CONSENSUS.

LOYAL
I REMAIN FAITHFUL TO THE COMMITMENTS I MAKE TO OTHERS.

METHODICAL
I AM ORDERLY IN ACTION, THOUGHT, AND EXPRESSION.

MODEST
I PLAY DOWN WHAT I AM CAPABLE OF DOING.

OPEN TO CHANGE
I CONSIDER DIFFERENT PERSPECTIVES, IDEAS, AND OPINIONS.

OPTION ORIENTED
I LOOK FOR AND SUGGEST DIFFERENT WAYS OF DOING THINGS.

PERSEVERING
I MAINTAIN THE SAME COURSE OF ACTION IN SPITE OF OBSTACLES.

PERSUASIVE
I URGE, INFLUENCE, AND CONVINCE OTHERS.

PRINCIPLED
I FOLLOW CERTAIN RULES OF RIGHT CONDUCT.

QUICK TO ACT
I GET THINGS STARTED WITHOUT DELAY.

RESERVED
I PRACTICE SELF-RESTRAINT IN EXPRESSING THOUGHTS AND FEELINGS.

RISK TAKING
I TAKE CHANCES ON LOSSES IN PURSUIT OF HIGH GAINS.

SELF CONFIDENT
I BELIEVE IN MY OWN POWERS AND STRENGTHS.

SOCIABLE
I ENGAGE EASILY IN GROUP CONVERSATIONS AND ACTIVITIES.

SUPPORTIVE
I GIVE ENCOURAGEMENT AND HELP TO OTHERS.

TOLERANT
I RESPECT DIFFERENCES, EVEN WHEN I DON'T AGREE.

TRUSTING
I PLACE MY FAITH IN OTHERS.

WRITE YOUR TOP 3 STRENGTHS AND THEIR DEFINITIONS IN THIS BOX.

1

2

3

*STRENGTHS PORTRAIT USED WITH PERMISSION BY CORESTRENGTHS.COM (CHECK OUT PAGE 223 FOR MORE).

YOU ARE THOSE

WHO HAVE STOOD BY ME IN MY TRIALS.

LUKE 22:28

FREEWAY

WHAT AM I LEARNING ABOUT MYSELF?

ABOUT GOD?

ARE YOU READY TO SHARE WHAT YOU'RE LEARNING
WITH SOMEONE?

[ ] ABSOLUTELY!

[ ] I'M REALLY NERVOUS ABOUT SHARING ... BUT I WILL.

[ ] NOT YET, BUT SOON.

[ ] NO WAY.

FROM YOUR HEART, WRITE A ONE-LINE PRAYER TO GOD.

SHARE

MEET WITH YOUR FRIENDS AND GO THROUGH THE
GROUP QUESTIONS TOGETHER.

GROUP QUESTIONS
STEP 2: DISCOVERY

If any of you lacks wisdom, you should ask God, who gives generously
to all without finding fault, and it will be given to you.

James 1:5 NIV

1. Take some time to discuss the pre-work: what you filled out, what you
think, how you feel about it, and what changes—if any—you'd like to make in
your life as you move toward freedom. What did you learn about yourself by
doing the reading and exercises this week?

PLAY THE DVD OR STREAM THE VIDEO ONLINE AT
SECONDCHANCE.ORG/MYFREEWAY

2. How do you feel when you're looking for something? Excited? Frustrated?

3. Have you ever looked for something that you really weren't that interested
in finding? How is that different from looking for something that you were
truly interested in finding?

4. Mike makes the observation that pain hides in our lives the same way the butter was hiding from him in the fridge. He said that we have to go looking for the root of our pain in order for us to deal with it in a healthy way. Do you agree? Disagree?

5. Mike gives some examples of how he unintentionally hurts others. In the film he says, "I knew I was a neat freak, but I had no idea how my neatfreakness was impacting my family." Have you ever experienced that with someone else?

6. Who can you talk to that you trust to help you discover your blind spots and their impact on others? Put another way: Who in your life do you trust to help you find the butter?

7. How will this journey of discovery help you become more free?

OPTIONAL GROUP ACTIVITY

Have each one in your group pass his or her workbook to another group member. Each group member should write a secret encouragement to that person somewhere in the workbook.

JUMP IN

LET'S TRY SOME STUFF THIS WEEK!

NOTICE YOUR EMOTIONS

This week, when you feel negative emotions creeping in, try to identify what's happening around you. See if you can identify some key triggers. Write them down.

DO SOMETHING YOU'VE BEEN SCARED TO DO

OK. So we all have those things we've been dreading and putting off. Maybe it's a difficult phone call. Or an apology. Or finally asking for help. Take thirty minutes sometime this week and load up as many yucky, ugly, and difficult things as possible and check them off your list.

CREATE YOUR "MY FREEWAY" ACCOUNT AT
SECONDCHANCE.ORG/MYFREEWAY
FOR DAILY DEVOTIONS, DOWNLOADS & VIDEOS

REMEMBER

JOURNAL, SCRIBBLE, & DOODLE YOUR THOUGHTS.

DOODLE HERE

HOW ARE THINGS GOING SO FAR?

SHARE WHAT YOU'RE LEARNING
WITH YOUR FRIENDS.

TWITTER   INSTAGRAM   FACEBOOK

#MYFREEWAY

OWNE

RSHIP

MAKING A COURAGEOUS DECISION TO TAKE PERSONAL
RESPONSIBILITY FOR OUR LIVES.

PREPARE

A SHORT INTRODUCTION TO A BIG IDEA.

STEP 3
OWNERSHIP

It was a silver four-door Hyundai Sonata with a dark grey fabric interior. The midsize rental was forty-nine dollars a day, plus the full-coverage insurance and a prepaid tank of gas. I jumped into the driver's seat, turned the key, and drove like a moronic madman down the Jane Addams Memorial Tollway.

Those two days in Chicago I careened into oily puddles, slammed on the brakes just for kicks, maxed the RPM gauge into the brightest red zone, and carelessly tossed my McDonald's cheeseburger wrappers into the backseat. I wiped my muddy Skechers on the fuzzy floor mats, splattered Coke on the center console, and sneezed directly onto the steering wheel … twice. I brought a level of anarchy, stupidity, and foulness to that four-door Hyundai that no rental car should ever be subjected to. Though what did I care, right? The car wasn't mine, and I was free and clear of all responsibility.

At the end of my two-day adventure, I flipped the keys to the Hertz attendant, said, "Thanks a bunch!" and flew back home to San Diego. No harm, no foul. The universal truth on display here: we treat what we rent differently than we treat what we own.

On our path to freedom, nothing unlocks more opportunity in our lives than the basic act of taking personal responsibility. No matter what has happened, either positive or negative, you get to decide what life looks like from here on out. Those painful things that happened in your past aren't your fault, but they are your responsibility. Sour lemons still come with some delicious and refreshing options if we're willing to take ownership of our life's lemonade stand.

Our liberator asks us to bravely live the un-lived life within and to stop believing the lie that we are damaged, done, or dead. Three simple words give us chain-busting freedom over our pasts:

"I. Own. It."

Dr. Seuss once poetically waxed, "You have brains in your head, you have feet in your shoes, you can steer yourself in any direction you choose." The fact is, no one else will live your story for you, and no one else is going to take your place. It belongs fully to you. Your actions, decisions, beliefs, and next steps are your responsibility.

This view empowers us to deal with the world the way it is, not the way we wish it was. And no matter how loudly we protest and stomp our feet or how many hissy-fit complaints we make, our history is our history—and my friend, it ain't changing.

When we fail to take ownership of our lives, the greatest enemy of our freedom is not the obvious abusive alcoholic father, that jerk who stabbed us in the back, or even the devil. For most, the enemy is far more dangerous than those others could ever be. "We have met the enemy and he is us," comic Walt Kelley quipped with perfect clarity. Tragically, our past hurts teach us how to hurt ourselves over and over again. It becomes a vicious, self-destructive cycle. Yet ownership isn't about blame for where the hurts came from; it's about taking responsibility for where we go from here.

And the great news of the gospel is that we don't have to point the finger or blame anyone anymore. By the way, that includes blaming yourself. Jesus's death and resurrection taught us that the cross powerfully conquers all victimhood. His enemies spit on him, his best friends sold him out, the mob nailed him to a wooden cross, but Jesus wasn't about to whine or point a finger. Christ's grave-busting return means we don't have to live like a gloomy Eeyore or have our life's soundtrack be some depressing Radiohead song.

We cannot un-see what we've seen or un-live what we've lived. We can, however—with the strength of the One who conquers death—move forward.

And so maybe we need to step outside, get some fresh air, and remind ourselves once again of whom we truly want to be. Jesus won't force you to take responsibility. He isn't bossy or rude like that. He just makes us a deal and says, "If you're ready, I'll trade that four-door Hyundai rental for a life that belongs to you."

EXPLORE

EXERCISES TO HELP YOU EXPLORE YOUR STORY.

I CAN ADMIT...

(ADMIT SOMETHING FUN)

(ADMIT SOMETHING PERSONAL)

(ADMIT SOMETHING THAT'S HARD TO SAY)

> BUT IF WE OWN UP TO OUR SINS, GOD SHOWS THAT HE IS FAITHFUL & JUST BY FORGIVING US OF OUR SINS.
>
> 1 JOHN 1:9

SHARE IT ONLINE?

#MYFREEWAY

IF YOUR LIFE WAS A CAR, HOW DO YOU TREAT IT?

 CHECK THOSE THAT APPLY:

OWNING RENTING BORROWING LEASING STEALING

EXPLAIN YOUR ANSWER IN THE BOX.

WHICH DIRECTION DO YOU WANT TO GO?

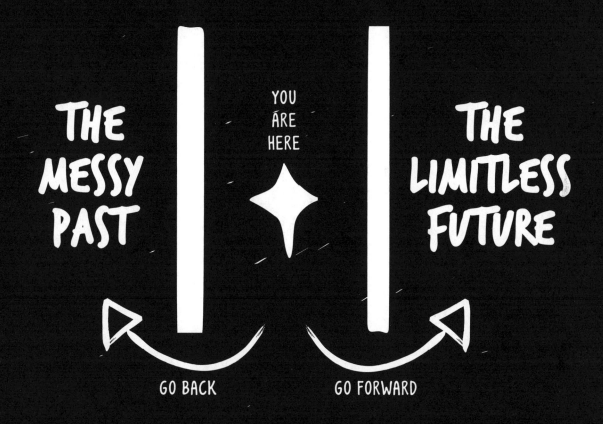

THE MESSY PAST

YOU ARE HERE

THE LIMITLESS FUTURE

GO BACK

GO FORWARD

EXPLAIN YOUR ANSWER IN THE BOX.

YOU CAN'T BLAME YOUR WAY TO FREEDOM.

FREEWAY

WHAT DOES TAKING RESPONSIBILITY FOR YOUR LIFE LOOK LIKE?

- -

- -

- -

- -

HOW DOES THIS LEAD TO FREEDOM?

- -

- -

- -

- -

WHAT ARE THE MOST COMMON WAYS THAT YOU HURT OTHERS?

(CIRCLE THE ONES THAT APPLY)

I DEMAND THAT MY NEEDS BE MET BY OTHERS.

I USE BLAME AND SHAME TO EMOTIONALLY HURT OTHERS.

I LABEL OTHERS WITH MY NEGATIVE TRAITS.

I MAKE DECISIONS WITHOUT REGARD TO THE CONSEQUENCES.

I PRETEND TO AGREE WITH OTHERS TO GET WHAT I WANT.

I EXPRESS NEGATIVITY IN INDIRECT AND PASSIVE WAYS.

I USE INDIRECT AND EVASIVE COMMUNICATION TO AVOID CONFLICT.

I WITHHOLD EXPRESSIONS OF APPRECIATION.

ANY OTHER WAYS?

HOW DO YOU JUSTIFY THAT BEHAVIOR?

WHAT ARE THE MOST COMMON WAYS THAT YOU HURT YOURSELF?

(CIRCLE THE ONES THAT APPLY)

I MINIMIZE OR DENY HOW I TRULY FEEL.

I MASK MY PAIN IN ANGER, HUMOR, OR ISOLATION.

I AM EMBARRASSED TO RECEIVE RECOGNITION, PRAISE, OR GIFTS.

I ACCEPT SEXUAL ATTENTION WHEN I REALLY WANT LOVE.

I AM AFRAID TO EXPRESS MY OPINIONS WHEN THEY DIFFER FROM THOSE OF OTHERS.

I HAVE TROUBLE SETTING HEALTHY PRIORITIES.

I AM EXTREMELY LOYAL, REMAINING IN HARMFUL SITUATIONS TOO LONG.

I AVOID EMOTIONAL, PHYSICAL, OR SEXUAL INTIMACY TO KEEP MY DISTANCE.

I BELIEVE DISPLAYS OF EMOTION ARE A SIGN OF WEAKNESS.

ANY OTHER WAYS?

- -

HOW DO YOU JUSTIFY THAT BEHAVIOR?

- -

- -

I HAVE HEARD THERE ARE TROUBLES OF MORE

THAN ONE KIND. SOME COME FROM AHEAD. SOME

COME FROM BEHIND. BUT I'VE BROUGHT A BIG BAT,

I'M ALL READY, YOU SEE. NOW MY TROUBLES ARE

GOING TO HAVE TROUBLES WITH ME!

DR. SEUSS

FREEWAY

WHAT AM I LEARNING ABOUT MYSELF?

- -

- -

ABOUT GOD?

- -

- -

ARE YOU READY TO SHARE WHAT YOU'RE LEARNING
WITH SOMEONE?

[ ] ABSOLUTELY!

[ ] I'M REALLY NERVOUS ABOUT SHARING ... BUT I WILL.

[ ] NOT YET, BUT SOON.

[ ] NO WAY.

FROM YOUR HEART, WRITE A ONE-LINE PRAYER TO GOD.

- -

SHARE

MEET WITH YOUR FRIENDS AND GO THROUGH THE
GROUP QUESTIONS TOGETHER.

GROUP QUESTIONS
STEP 3: OWNERSHIP

When I was a child, I spoke and thought and reasoned as a child.
But when I grew up, I put away childish things.

1 Corinthians 13:11 NLT

1. Take some time to discuss the pre-work: what you filled out, what you think, how you feel about it, and what changes—if any—you'd like to make in your life as you move toward freedom. What did you learn about yourself by doing the reading and exercises this week?

 **PLAY THE DVD OR STREAM THE VIDEO ONLINE AT SECONDCHANCE.ORG/MYFREEWAY**

2. We blame and complain for a reason. What do we get out of it? What do you tend to whine about?

3. How does complaining about something get in the way of us owning our problem, circumstance, or situation? Explain.

4. What are some things you've discovered so far in these past few weeks that would be healthy for you to own? What would it look like to take personal responsibility for your life right now?

5. Mike uses the analogy of renting versus owning. How does owning our own problems help us in our spiritual journey and our relationships with God and others?

6. God paid a high price for you. Do you believe that you are a good investment? Explain.

OPTIONAL GROUP ACTIVITY

Have everyone identify the most expensive thing that they have in their possession. It could be a phone, a pair of shoes or a watch. Discuss how well you take care of that item versus other items.

JUMP IN

LET'S TRY SOME STUFF THIS WEEK!

PLANT SOMETHING

This week, plant some seeds and grow something from scratch. It can be a vegetable or a tree or some flowers. Use it as a reminder that if something is going to grow, you must take responsibility for it.

PRACTICE SAYING SORRY

Let's practice saying sorry this week. Set a daily goal of saying "I'm Sorry," and see if you can hit it. Find as many opportunities as possible to take personal responsibility for your actions.

CATCH YOUR COMPLAINTS

When you are tempted to start whining or complaining about something, pause for five seconds. Catch that negative thought and then replace the frustration you feel by identifying something you are thankful for in life. It can be big or small. Practice gratitude.

CREATE YOUR "MY FREEWAY" ACCOUNT AT
SECONDCHANCE.ORG/MYFREEWAY
FOR DAILY DEVOTIONS, DOWNLOADS & VIDEOS

REMEMBER

JOURNAL, SCRIBBLE, & DOODLE YOUR THOUGHTS.

DOODLE HERE

GOD'S LOVE WILL ALWAYS FIND A WAY INTO OUR DARKNESS.

FREEWAY

STEP 4

FORGIV

ENESS

SURRENDERING THE CHASE FOR JUSTICE AND ALLOWING GOD
TO RELEASE US FROM OUR PAIN.

PREPARE

A SHORT INTRODUCTION TO A BIG IDEA.

STEP 4
FORGIVENESS

I recently heard about radical "birders" who spend their entire lives chasing after the most elusive birds in the world. They don't pursue those run-of-the-mill talking parrots or French-fry-eating pigeons camped outside Burger King. These avid bird chasers diligently search the forests of Japan for the prized Copper Pheasant with its rich, coppery chestnut plumage and daydream about spotting a male rosefinch resting in weedy plants.

Birders pack duffle bags full of telescopes, travel to far-off lands, and sacrifice everything to study the patterns of the mythological Green Kingfisher. Their lives are fully consumed with the remote possibility of spotting the world's most unseen creatures. Whether these bird-watchers admit it or not, their lives are a constant chase for a moment that will most likely never come.

Pain often puts us on a chase similar to the ones the crazy birders are on. Our minds are flooded with the slight possibility of finding those hard-to-locate answers to our suffering. We wake up in the morning thinking, *Maybe today is the day it all makes sense.* We hunt and chase the most elusive question known to hurting hearts: the "why."

Why did this happen?

Why did God take him so soon?

Why do I keep doing the same things over and over?

Why don't they love me anymore?

Suffering always brings overstuffed suitcases full of questions that we lug around on our global search for understanding. But these slippery answers rarely arrive.

Loss, abuse, betrayal, and our frequent trips back to our destructive addictions have left us baffled, bewildered, and confused. Yet real freedom is rarely found by spotting the stealthy "why"—but rather by letting our stories be captured by the plain and obvious "who."

Who will you trust with your pain?

Who loves you with reckless abandon?

Who will wipe every tear away?

Who can trade your heart of stone for a heart of flesh?

Who will bend down to kiss your face and take your hand?

And after all our failed attempts to make sense of our hurts, this "who" is asking us to finally surrender the "why" to God.

Only in Jesus do we find both the courage and the permission to admit that we've been wronged and have wronged others. In Jesus the crucified, we see the model of radical forgiveness that we are called to offer others and ourselves.

"Forgive them, for they know not what they do" were not just the dying words of a martyred Savior (Luke 23:24 ESV) but the clear pathway to finding everything we've been looking for. We don't need high-powered binoculars or telescopes in order to see that tomorrow's freedom is found in today's white-flag surrender to him.

Sadly, bitterness and resentment lock us up in our very own birdcage. This prison holds us captive with the belief that we've been treated unfairly and that the world is against us. It throws seeds of tension into every aspect of our lives. The slights, insults, unintentional hurts, and epic injustices become our all-consuming pet projects as we hunt a solution to right the wrongs.

But we can stop the chase if we want to. If you're tired you can find rest in forgiveness. We've all searched too many forests, trees, and weedy plants for answers. Jesus sees how weary we've become.

Let go. Seriously, let go of it all. It probably sounds too easy, but surrender every messy bit of it. Release back into the wild every poisoned thought, every idea of revenge, and every ounce of hatred. Bitterness doesn't belong to you anymore. It belongs to the crucified Savior, and he wants it back. And though we live with fading scars and walk with a faint limp, those are simply echoes that remind us how strong we are and how far we've come.

Jesus promises to take care of all this stuff, and he doesn't need our assistance—only our hearts. Because two thousand years ago, a rooster crowed, and a man took on all the world's injustice, filth, abuse, and rottenness and said, "It is finished." And with that, forgiveness wins, and the elusive chase is over.

EXPLORE

EXERCISES TO HELP YOU EXPLORE YOUR STORY.

DRAW OUT THE THING YOU'RE HAVING A HARD TIME FORGIVING.

SKETCH OR WRITE AS MUCH DETAIL AS POSSIBLE.

CAN JESUS HELP YOU FORGIVE THIS PERSON OR SITUATION?

THE BIRD HUNT

JUST LIKE CHASING AN ELUSIVE BIRD, WHAT HARD-TO-FIND ANSWERS
HAVE YOU BEEN CHASING IN YOUR STORY? ANSWERS TO PAINFUL EVENTS?
BETRAYAL? EXPLANATIONS OF ABUSE? LOSS?

WRITE YOUR ANSWERS INSIDE THE BIRDS.

LIST WHAT MIGHT HAPPEN IF YOU TAKE THE RISK TO FORGIVE.

IT CAN BE POSITIVE OR NEGATIVE.

- -

- -

- -

- -

- -

- -

IS IT WORTH THE RISK?

[ ]   [ ]   [ ]

YES   NO   NOT SURE

SING A NEW TUNE!

YOU CAN'T START SINGING A NEW SONG UNTIL YOU STOP SINGING THE OLD TUNE. MAKE UP SOME OLD AND NEW SONG TITLES FOR YOUR LIFE. BE CREATIVE!!

NAME YOUR OLD SONG:

"   "

NAME YOUR NEW SONG:

"   "

SING A NEW SONG TO THE LORD!
SING IT EVERYWHERE AROUND THE WORLD.
PSALM 96:1 TLB

BLESSED ARE THOSE
WHO MAKE PEACE.

MATTHEW 5:9 ISV

WHITE FLAG
OF SURRENDER!!

WHAT DO YOU WANT TO COMPLETELY SURRENDER TO JESUS RIGHT NOW?
WRITE IT LOUD AND PROUD ON THE FLAG!!

LOVE BREAKS OUR FALL, GRACE CARRIES US HOME.

– BOB GOFF –

FREEWAY

WRITE A LETTER TO THE PERSON YOU'RE FORGIVING

GRAB MORE PAPER IF YOU NEED IT!

DEAR,

WRITE YOUR HOPES & DREAMS IN THE BOX BELOW.

 ON YELLOW STICKY NOTES, WRITE THE THINGS YOU REFUSE TO FORGIVE.

 NOW PLACE THOSE STICKY NOTES OVER THE BOX ABOVE.

CAN YOU SEE HOW BITTERNESS & RESENTMENT CAN DAMAGE YOUR FUTURE?

WHAT AM I LEARNING ABOUT MYSELF?

ABOUT GOD?

ARE YOU READY TO SHARE WHAT YOU'RE LEARNING
WITH SOMEONE?

[ ] ABSOLUTELY!

[ ] I'M REALLY NERVOUS ABOUT SHARING ... BUT I WILL.

[ ] NOT YET, BUT SOON.

[ ] NO WAY.

FROM YOUR HEART, WRITE A ONE-LINE PRAYER TO GOD.

SHARE

MEET WITH YOUR FRIENDS AND GO THROUGH THE
GROUP QUESTIONS TOGETHER.

GROUP QUESTIONS
STEP 4: FORGIVENESS

Do not judge, and you will not be judged. Do not condemn,
and you will not be condemned. Forgive, and you will be forgiven.

Luke 6:37 NIV

1. Take some time to discuss the pre-work: what you filled out, what you think, how you feel about it, and what changes—if any—you'd like to make in your life as you move toward freedom. What did you learn about yourself by doing the reading and exercises this week?

PLAY THE DVD OR STREAM THE VIDEO ONLINE AT SECONDCHANCE.ORG/MYFREEWAY

2. Define forgiveness. What does it mean to receive forgiveness from God, others, and yourself?

3. How is forgiveness different from excusing what people have done or just avoiding what people have done?

4. Mike shares a story about someone saying hurtful things about him behind his back and his daydreaming of getting revenge. Have you ever thought about how you could get someone back? Ever imagined having the perfect comeback line? Why does it feel so good to do that?

5. What are some things in your life that you need to surrender to God? How does not letting go or not forgiving actually hurt you in the meantime? Explain.

6. Why is it so difficult to forgive ourselves?

7. Which is more difficult for you: receiving forgiveness from God, from others, or from yourself? Are all three equally difficult?

OPTIONAL GROUP ACTIVITY

Take a moment and have everyone write the name of the person they need to forgive. Write the name in the workbook. Then pray as a group together for the courage to forgive.

JUMP IN

LET'S TRY SOME STUFF THIS WEEK!

HANDS OPEN

When you pray this week, turn your hands up to heaven. Let this be a simple form of physical surrender to God. Sure, it may look and feel a little funny, but it might help you release things to him.

BURNING CEREMONY

Get a small notebook or piece of paper. Write all your hurts, fears, failures, and ugly thoughts on the paper. Say whatever you want to say! Get it all out! Keep it as raw and honest as possible. And then find a quiet place. Pray a prayer to God, and then light the paper on fire as a symbolic way to show you're surrendering it all to him.

CREATE YOUR "MY FREEWAY" ACCOUNT AT
SECONDCHANCE.ORG/MYFREEWAY
FOR DAILY DEVOTIONS, DOWNLOADS & VIDEOS

REMEMBER

JOURNAL, SCRIBBLE, & DOODLE YOUR THOUGHTS.

DOODLE HERE

THERE IS NO GREATER AGONY THAN BEARING AN UNTOLD STORY INSIDE YOU.

– MAYA ANGELOU –

FREEWAY

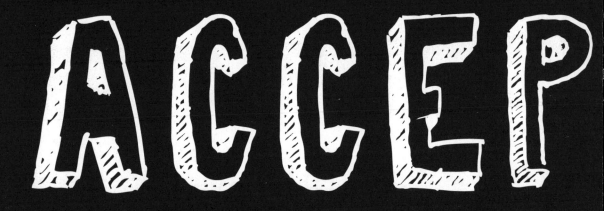

WHOLEHEARTEDLY EMBRACING OUR TRUE IDENTITY AND VALUE
IN BEING GOD'S BELOVED.

PREPARE

A SHORT INTRODUCTION TO A BIG IDEA.

STEP 5
ACCEPTANCE

It is located thirty minutes outside of Beijing, China. Western tourists have nicknamed it "Not Quite the Happiest Place on Earth." Buy your guest pass, slap on the sunscreen, grab your kids, and enter into a very "amusing" park.

For your first stop, head over to the dusty golf-ball-like structure that is eerily reminiscent of Epcot's Spaceship Earth. Pull out your camera and strike a pose with Minnie Mouse, whose red polka-dot dress is faded and frayed. Stroll past the paint-peeling splendor of Sleeping Beauty's castle, and step on board the malfunctioning Dumbo's Flying Elephant ride. As you exit, pick up a few cheap plastic souvenirs and a plagiarized copy of *Snow White and the Seven Dwarves.*

Though this Beijing destination clearly resembles a Walt Disney theme park, the Shijingshan Amusement Park is a fraudulent copy of the "happiest place on Earth." Breaking hundreds of international copyright laws, the owners have poorly re-created Walt's original vision. To the untrained eye it may seem legit, but those who have been to a Disney theme park know it's an uninspired copy of the real thing.

Knockoffs are not new, are they? Twenty-dollar Rolex watches, candy cigarettes with fake sugar smoke, and pirated copies of the Lord of the Rings trilogy show up every day. We have become so accustomed to counterfeits that we have even allowed our own lives to become an acceptable forgery. Our feelings of inadequacy have convinced us to mask our human imperfections in our own Mickey Mouse costume. We play the role of Super Mom or Mr. Got-It-Together Guy and dress up in fake smiles and surgically enhanced bodies. We are trapped in a dark castle of people-pleasing and float into a small world after all.

Somewhere in our story we believed that we were flawed. We listened to the lying liars and morphed into characters of a devilish fairy tale. Our dreams of being fully loved have broken down, and our closest relationships malfunction. On the outside we pretend we're so put together, but in our hearts we know it is slowly coming undone—and as poet Henry David Thoreau wrote, "Most men live lives of quiet desperation and go to their grave with the song still in them."

What the world has tried to silence over the years, Jesus asks us to now sing. He reminds us that you and I are the "pearl of great price" and the magnificent "treasure hidden in the field." He longs to dress us in his glory and make us his princes and princesses in his enchanted kingdom. His pursuit is wild and zealous, and the only reasonable response to this sort of infatuated, punch-drunk lover is to accept his offer to be his and his alone.

And when we finally believe that God accepts us, we might take the risk to even accept ourselves. How scandalous would it be to finally have the audacity to be our own friend and see, as Brennan Manning said, "how glorious the splendor of a human heart that trusts that it is loved." We could be safe in our skin, and the quiet desperation of striving to measure up is no more. We no longer just believe in God; we believe in us, too. This is complete acceptance. Though this is not easy, is it? I should know. As I type these words, I still fight for this to be true in my own life. Each day the accuser wiggles into my thoughts and reminds me that I am a fraud and that my so-called "devotion to God" is laughable. Interestingly enough, the accuser's voice sounds eerily like my own.

So what if we are total hypocrites? And so what if people see that we are a sizzling hot mess and we bleach our teeth and liposuction our thighs? So what if our family operates like a busted-up Dumbo's Flying Elephant ride and we're six inches shy of life's height requirement? So what if we are the frauds, fakers, and crowned leaders of a gang of hypocrites?

Let our accuser sling the lies, indict our name, and denounce our faithless hearts. Blacklist us, shame us, and let our good deeds be shown for what they are: filthy rags stained with blood. For no matter what the accuser impeaches us on, we will be vindicated by Jesus's audacious and unrelenting grace. He crushes judgment with his great love.

Throw out your fading costumes, and hand back your cheap plastic souvenirs. Walk away from the cover-up, and step into your royal inheritance. For it is not what we see, or what we feel, or what we did, or what they say … but it is the truth of who we know ourselves to be in Jesus. We're not perfect—just perfectly loved.

EXPLORE

EXERCISES TO HELP YOU EXPLORE YOUR STORY.

FIND THE BEAUTY IN THE BROKEN

THE NEGATIVE SITUATION OR EVENT	THE POSITIVES THAT CAME OUT OF IT

BEHOLD, I AM MAKING ALL THINGS NEW. – REVELATION 21:5 NASB

WHO AM I?

CHECK THOSE THAT APPLY.

VICTIM

STUDENT

BOYFRIEND/
GIRLFRIEND

DIVORCED

SUCCESSFUL

ARTIST

PARENT

BUSINESSPERSON

BELOVED

A PUSHOVER

SPORTS FAN

ATTRACTIVE

☐ SPOUSE

☐ SINGLE

☐ LOST

☐ A FAILURE

☐ HAS-BEEN

☐ FELON

☐ SEXUAL

☐ RELIGIOUS

☐ LIFE OF
THE PARTY

☐ A MISTAKE

☐ OTHER:

WHAT IDENTITY DO YOU ALIGN WITH THE MOST?

WHO ARE YOU IN GOD'S EYES?

WHICH STATEMENTS DO YOU BELIEVE ARE TRUE ABOUT YOU?

CIRCLE THOSE THAT YOU THINK APPLY.

I WISH I WAS SOMEONE ELSE.

I SHOULD BE FURTHER ALONG IN MY LIFE BY NOW.

I DON'T MAKE ENOUGH EFFORT WITH OTHER PEOPLE.

I DON'T EXERCISE AS MUCH AS I SHOULD.

I SHOULD DO MORE.

I'M ALWAYS DOING THE WRONG THING AT THE WRONG TIME.

I COULD DO BETTER AT MY JOB.

I'M NOT VERY ATTRACTIVE.

I'M A TALKER, NOT A LISTENER.

I'M INVISIBLE TO OTHERS.

MY FRIENDS ARE SO MUCH BETTER THAN I AM.

I FEEL FAKE.

I SHOULD DO
MORE FOR GOD.

I DON'T MAKE
ENOUGH TIME
FOR THE KIDS.

OTHER PEOPLE
ARE A LOT MORE
SUCCESSFUL
AND CREATIVE
THAN ME.

I'M NOT SMART.

I DON'T MAKE
ENOUGH TIME
FOR MY SPOUSE.

I'M KINDA LAZY.

I MAKE
PROMISES TO
MYSELF AND
BREAK THEM.

I COULD
REALLY LOSE
SOME WEIGHT.

I'M A PEOPLE
PLEASER.

IT'S OK TO ACKNOWLEDGE YOUR
FEELINGS, BUT YOU DON'T ALWAYS
HAVE TO AGREE WITH THEM. DON'T
EMPOWER YOUR INNER CRITIC. GIVE
YOURSELF SOME GRACE.

OTHER:

- - - - - - - - -

DO YOU THINK YOU'RE BEING
TOO HARD ON YOURSELF?

☐   ☐   ☐
YES   NO   MAYBE

MY LIFE
DOESN'T MATTER.

BE JOYFUL IN HOPE, PATIENT IN AFFLICTION,

FAITHFUL IN PRAYER.

ROMANS 12:12 NIV

FREEWAY

LIST SOME SIMPLE WAYS YOU CAN SHOW YOURSELF COMPASSION.

 ---------------------------------

DO YOU THINK IT'S IMPORTANT TO DO THIS? WHY?

HOW DO YOU FEEL...

1. WHEN YOU WAKE UP IN THE A.M.? _ _ _ _ _ _ _ _ _ _ _ _ _ _ _ _

2. WHEN YOU MAKE A MISTAKE? _ _ _ _ _ _ _ _ _ _ _ _ _ _ _ _

3. WHEN YOU HURT PEOPLE? _ _ _ _ _ _ _ _ _ _ _ _ _ _ _

4. WHEN YOU ARE LATE TO A MEETING? _ _ _ _ _ _ _ _ _ _ _ _

5. WHEN YOU RUN OVER A CAT? _ _ _ _ _ _ _ _ _ _ _ _ _ _

6. WHEN YOU HAVE RELATIONAL DIFFICULTIES? _ _ _ _ _ _ _ _ _ _

7. WHEN YOUR JOKE ISN'T FUNNY? _ _ _ _ _ _ _ _ _ _ _ _ _

8. WHEN YOU UNDERPERFORM AT WORK? _ _ _ _ _ _ _ _ _ _ _

9. WHEN YOU LOSE YOUR TEMPER? _ _ _ _ _ _ _ _ _ _ _ _ _

10. WHEN YOU SIN? _ _ _ _ _ _ _ _ _ _ _ _ _ _ _ _ _

HOW DOES GOD FEEL...

1. WHEN YOU WAKE UP IN THE A.M.? _ _ _ _ _ _ _ _ _ _ _ _ _ _ _ _ _

2. WHEN YOU MAKE A MISTAKE? _ _ _ _ _ _ _ _ _ _ _ _ _ _ _ _

3. WHEN YOU HURT PEOPLE? _ _ _ _ _ _ _ _ _ _ _ _ _ _ _ _

4. WHEN YOU ARE LATE TO A MEETING? _ _ _ _ _ _ _ _ _ _ _ _ _

5. WHEN YOU RUN OVER A CAT? _ _ _ _ _ _ _ _ _ _ _ _ _ _ _

6. WHEN YOU HAVE RELATIONAL DIFFICULTIES? _ _ _ _ _ _ _ _ _ _ _

7. WHEN YOUR JOKE ISN'T FUNNY? _ _ _ _ _ _ _ _ _ _ _ _ _ _

8. WHEN YOU UNDERPERFORM AT WORK? _ _ _ _ _ _ _ _ _ _ _ _

9. WHEN YOU LOSE YOUR TEMPER? _ _ _ _ _ _ _ _ _ _ _ _ _

10. WHEN YOU SIN? _ _ _ _ _ _ _ _ _ _ _ _ _ _ _ _

TRUE OR FALSE?

YOU'RE NOT LOVED CUZ YOU'RE VALUABLE, YOU'RE
VALUABLE CUZ YOU'RE LOVED BY GOD.

TRUE   FALSE

WHAT DOES THIS MEAN TO YOU?

WHAT SHALL WE SAY ABOUT SUCH WONDERFUL THINGS AS THESE? IF GOD IS FOR US, WHO CAN EVER BE AGAINST US?

ROMANS 8:31 NLT

FREEWAY

Don't Believe Everything You Think About Yourself.

Freeway

THE PEOPLE WHO LOVE ME...

- -

- -

- -

- -

THE PEOPLE WHO I LOVE...

- -

- -

- -

- -

EVERY TIME I PUT GOD IN A BOX,

I'M LEFT SWEEPING UP THE PIECES

OF SHREDDED CARDBOARD.

JOSH RIEBOCK

FREEWAY

WHAT IS YOUR NEW NAME BEFORE GOD?

CUT IT OUT AND PIN IT TO YOUR SHIRT.

I WILL ALSO GIVE THAT PERSON A WHITE STONE WITH A NEW NAME
WRITTEN ON IT, KNOWN ONLY TO THE ONE WHO RECEIVES IT.
- REVELATION 2:17 NIV -

*SPACE FOR NEGATIVE COMMENTS & THOUGHTS!

*NOW CUT OUT A WHITE PIECE OF PAPER AND GLUE IT TO THIS PAGE. WRITE THE WORD *GRACE* IN REALLY BIG LETTERS ON THIS PAGE.

REMEMBER WHO YOU ARE!

I AM HIS BELOVED
JEREMIAH 31:3

I AM A CHILD OF GOD
1 JOHN 3:1

I AM HEAVEN'S POETRY
EPHESIANS 2:10

I AM FORGIVEN
1 PETER 2:24

I AM WHOLE IN CHRIST
COLOSSIANS 2:10

I AM NEVER ALONE
DEUTERONOMY 31:8

I AM AN EXQUISITE FRAGRANCE
2 CORINTHIANS 2:15

I AM FREE
GALATIANS 5:1

TO BE NOBODY-BUT-YOURSELF — IN A WORLD

THAT'S DOING ITS BEST, NIGHT AND DAY, TO MAKE

YOU EVERYBODY ELSE — IS TO FIGHT THE HARDEST

BATTLE WHICH ANY HUMAN BEING CAN FIGHT;

AND NEVER STOP.

E.E. CUMMINGS

FREEWAY

SKETCH A PICTURE OF YOURSELF

1. CIRCLE YOUR FAVORITE PHYSICAL FEATURE
2. PUT AN X ON YOUR LEAST FAVORITE PHYSICAL FEATURE

HOW GLORIOUS THE SPLENDOR OF A HUMAN HEART THAT TRUSTS THAT IT IS LOVED.

- BRENNAN MANNING -

FREEWAY

WHAT AM I LEARNING ABOUT MYSELF?

- -

- -

ABOUT GOD?

- -

- -

ARE YOU READY TO SHARE WHAT YOU'RE LEARNING WITH SOMEONE?

[ ] ABSOLUTELY!

[ ] I'M REALLY NERVOUS ABOUT SHARING ... BUT I WILL.

[ ] NOT YET, BUT SOON.

[ ] NO WAY.

FROM YOUR HEART, WRITE A ONE-LINE PRAYER TO GOD.

- -

SHARE

MEET WITH YOUR FRIENDS AND GO THROUGH THE
GROUP QUESTIONS TOGETHER.

GROUP QUESTIONS
STEP 5: ACCEPTANCE

He rescued me because he delighted in me.

Psalm 18:19 NIV

1. Take some time to discuss the pre-work: what you filled out, what you think, how you feel about it, and what changes—if any—you'd like to make in your life as you move toward freedom. What did you learn about yourself by doing the reading and exercises this week?

PLAY THE DVD OR STREAM THE VIDEO ONLINE AT
SECONDCHANCE.ORG/MYFREEWAY

2. How might we treat ourselves and others differently if we realized that everyone was a unique creation of God?

3. When do you feel unlovable? Unworthy? Do you struggle with self acceptance?

4. Mike tells the story about how his dad would show his love by placing a little yellow note in Mike's sack lunch each day. What are some ways you might not realize that God shows you that he loves you every day?

5. Why is it so easy to compromise who we are and become people pleasers? Do you sometimes do this in your life?

6. Do you think accepting yourself is a prerequisite to being able to receive love from God and others? Explain your answer.

7. How can you embrace and love your imperfections and flaws?

OPTIONAL GROUP ACTIVITY

Get a pencil. Set a timer for sixty seconds. In your workbook, quickly draw the Muppet that you think that you're most like. Now show your drawings to one another and have people guess which Muppet you've drawn.

JUMP IN

LET'S TRY SOME STUFF THIS WEEK!

YOUR SECRET NAME

God likes to hand out new names. Simon to Peter. Saul to Paul. Jacob to Israel. In Revelation 2, God talks about a white stone with a new name on it. It's a name just for you. What is your best sense of God's special nickname for you? Use a Sharpie pen and write this name on a rock. Now put it someplace special.

STOP STINKING THINKING

This week watch your thoughts. When they become negative or destructive, consider where these thoughts are coming from. Pause. Take a breath. Ask yourself: Is it from God? Or is it from the enemy? Is it helpful, or does it bring you down?

CREATE YOUR "MY FREEWAY" ACCOUNT AT
SECONDCHANCE.ORG/MYFREEWAY
FOR DAILY DEVOTIONS, DOWNLOADS & VIDEOS

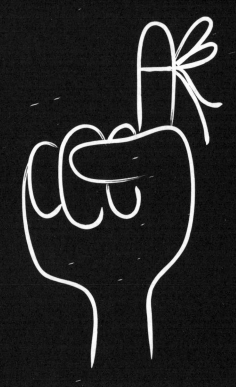

REMEMBER

JOURNAL, SCRIBBLE, & DOODLE YOUR THOUGHTS.

DOODLE HERE

He rescued me because he delighted in me.

Psalm 18:19

Freeway

DOM

DISCOVERING THAT OUR PAIN HAS A PURPOSE AND THAT NOTHING IS WASTED IN GOD'S KINGDOM.

PREPARE

A SHORT INTRODUCTION TO A BIG IDEA.

STEP 6
FREEDOM

In 1494, the semicolon was born. Fathered by the Italian printer Aldus Manutius, this quirky little punctuation mark has lived quite a marvelous life. It has appeared in great literature, separates our friends' addresses in our emails, and is a whimsical emoticon to show that someone is "winking." No one could have predicted back in 1494 the influential life the semicolon would live.

But it makes sense, considering its original point for coming into the world. For writers, a semicolon is applied when a sentence might have ended but continued on. Instead of closing the thought, the author went forward with one more additional idea.

God uses semicolons freely in our stories. As he writes our next chapters, he transitions the painful passages of our pasts into a beautiful future. We thought the sentence was done, but oh no—he was just transitioning.

What a thrill it is to know that God is grabbing his favorite Montblanc fountain pen and is outlining a Pulitzer Prize winner with you as the lead character. If you thought Hemingway, Steinbeck, and Dickens could craft a fine sentence, wait till you see what the author of all stories is scripting for you.

Every tear you cried and every desperate prayer you prayed has been for this moment. God promises us that nothing is wasted. Seriously—nothing. Everything you have faced has brought you to this moment to embrace your profound mission: to love the loveless and help God patch up the broken hearts. And instead of regretting where we've been, we now give thanks for where we're going. And like the prophet Isaiah, you will know this to be true:

> He has anointed me to bring good news to the poor. He has sent me to repair broken hearts and to declare to those who are held captive and bound in prison, "Be free from your imprisonment!"
> (Isa. 61:1–3, The Voice)

All that you thought was ugly and useless will become the gift that you bring to the world. Your pain will be your platform—because now your heart is softer and wiser and more unconditional. Wounded hearts will find safety and comfort in your friendship. Concentration-camp survivor Viktor Frankl once said, "I grasped the meaning of the greatest secret that human poetry and human thought and belief have to impart: The salvation of man is through love and in love."

But sometimes running forward into the miracle of our second chance is as scary as the work it took to finally find it. You will bump into the well-intentioned second-chance safety analysts who will explain to you, "It's not time," or "You're not qualified," or who will chuckle, "Don't be all crazy now. You can't do that." They prefer to use question marks and periods in their stories instead of God's supernatural semicolons.

Oh my freedom fighter, you will feel pain again, but this time you'll be ready. Critics will explain to you why you can't, but you don't have to listen to them. Just go grab the hands of friends who accept your past, support your present, and cheer your future. The dying world needs more wild ideas, and you've got nothing to lose and everything to gain. Jesus smiles when we courageously grab hold of our second chance.

You and I have been rescued to become rescuers. That is freedom's job offer. And in a stunning plot twist that you never saw coming, all this has never really been about you in the first place, but about him ... and them. The journey of freedom isn't just about us breaking free but about joining the soul liberation front.

Right now, there is another coming-home party being planned. So blow up the mylar balloons and load up on whizzers, kazoos, and fiesta maracas, for we are getting ready for more prodigals' arrivals. Get the band together, and put your dancing shoes on. For you, my beautifully broken soul, will now be leading the ragamuffin parade and will march the captives from their prison cells. Why? Because you know the free way and have discovered what all of us are searching for. You've met the heavenly liberator and realize that the ending to every story God writes is freedom.

EXPLORE

EXERCISES TO HELP YOU EXPLORE YOUR STORY.

WHAT PARTS OF YOUR
STORY DO YOU THINK GO IN
THE TRASH CAN?

WHAT GOES ON THE
PLATFORM TO HELP OTHERS?

IS THERE ANYTHING YOU THINK
GOD CAN'T USE TO HELP OTHERS?

WHAT IS YOUR VISION?

MY VISION IS...

WHAT DO YOU DREAM ABOUT FOR YOUR LIFE?

WHAT ARE SOME NEXT STEPS YOU CAN TAKE NOW? + + + + + + +

WHAT DO YOU SEE FOR YOUR LIFE TEN YEARS FROM NOW?

HOW BIG ARE YOUR DREAMS?

S   M   L   XL

FIND YOUR JOY!

WHAT BRINGS YOU JOY?

1
2
3
4

WHAT ACTIVITIES REPLENISH YOU?

1
2
3
4

MAY THE GOD OF HOPE FILL YOU WITH ALL JOY AND PEACE AS YOU TRUST IN HIM...
ROMANS 13:15 NIV

TRACE YOUR HAND ON THIS PAGE

INSIDE THE OUTLINE OF YOUR HAND WRITE THINGS THAT THIS HAND COULD DO TO HELP AND SERVE OTHERS.

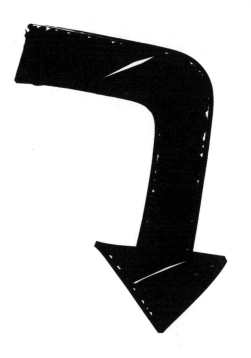

YOUR STORY IS MEANT FOR OTHERS!!

LIST THE TYPES OF PEOPLE WHO WOULD BE HELPED BY KNOWING YOUR STORY AND WHAT YOU LEARNED DURING TOUGH TIMES.

❋ 1 --

❋ 2 --

❋ 3 --

❋ 4 --

❋ NOW GO AND LOVE, SERVE AND SHARE YOUR LIFE WITH THESE FOLKS!!

WRITE SOME NAMES OF FRIENDS WHO NEED FREEDOM JUST LIKE YOU.

HOW COULD YOU BEST HELP THEM TO BE FREE?

OUR WOUNDED HEART AND OUR DEEPEST PAIN

IS ALWAYS THE STARTING PLACE FOR HELPING

HEAL THE WORLD.

FREEWAY

WHAT AM I LEARNING ABOUT MYSELF?

- -

- -

ABOUT GOD?

- -

- -

ARE YOU READY TO SHARE WHAT YOU'RE LEARNING
WITH SOMEONE?

[ ] ABSOLUTELY!

[ ] I'M REALLY NERVOUS ABOUT SHARING ... BUT I WILL.

[ ] NOT YET, BUT SOON.

[ ] NO WAY.

FROM YOUR HEART, WRITE A ONE-LINE PRAYER TO GOD.

- -

SHARE

MEET WITH YOUR FRIENDS AND GO THROUGH THE
GROUP QUESTIONS TOGETHER.

GROUP QUESTIONS
STEP 6: FREEDOM

It is for freedom that Christ has set us free. Stand firm, then, and do not let yourselves be burdened again by a yoke of slavery.

Galatians 5:1 NIV

1. Take some time to discuss the pre-work: what you filled out, what you think, how you feel about it, and what changes—if any—you'd like to make in your life as you move toward freedom. What did you learn about yourself by doing the reading and exercises this week?

 **PLAY THE DVD OR STREAM THE VIDEO ONLINE AT SECONDCHANCE.ORG/MYFREEWAY**

2. Mike shares a story about caterpillars and butterflies and how they never return back to the jar. What does it look like for us in our journey toward freedom to "return back to the jar"?

3. What prevents people from receiving a second chance and living a free life? Why do people reject freedom and choose to stay "stuck"?

4. As you move forward, how can you be intentional about not going back into the jar of captivity to your past habits, perspectives, hurts, and hurdles?

5. Over the course of the past weeks in which way do you think you've grown the most?

6. What's one way you can use your freedom to help others find freedom?

OPTIONAL GROUP ACTIVITY

1. Buy some helium-filled balloons. Hand a balloon to each person. Have everyone in your group write on the balloon what they want to be free from. Release the balloons together outside. Make sure to take a photo and tag it #myfreeway.

2. Plan some ways that you can continue to connect and share in each other's lives. Talk about some next steps as a group.

JUMP IN

LET'S TRY SOME STUFF THIS WEEK!

FREEWAY FIELD TRIP

Take some time this week and go back through your entire Freeway workbook. Review some of the Explore exercises and different things that you wrote down. Circle or highlight things that are key to your freedom.

START YOUR OWN GROUP

If you have enjoyed the Freeway experience, consider inviting some friends to do it with you. It can be as simple as inviting them over for coffee, asking them to meet for lunch at work, or meeting at the local park. It doesn't have to be fancy at all. Go for it!

SHARE YOUR STORY

We are all in this together! So let's share our stories. Share your thoughts, photos and what you learned online. Use the hashtag #myfreeway.

> CREATE YOUR "MY FREEWAY" ACCOUNT AT
> SECONDCHANCE.ORG/MYFREEWAY
> FOR DAILY DEVOTIONS, DOWNLOADS & VIDEOS

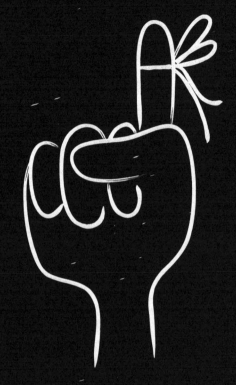

REMEMBER

JOURNAL, SCRIBBLE, & DOODLE YOUR THOUGHTS.

DOODLE HERE

ADVERSITY PREPARES ORDINARY PEOPLE FOR EXTRAORDINARY LIVES.

FREEWAY

THE
FINAL
WORDS

LOVE IS ALWAYS STRONGER THAN DEATH, AND
UNTO THAT LOVE YOU HAVE NOW RETURNED.
I ORDER YOU, O SLEEPER, TO AWAKE!
I DID NOT CREATE YOU TO BE HELD A PRISONER IN HELL.
RISE FROM THE DEAD, FOR I AM THE LIFE OF THE DEAD.
RISE UP, WORK OF MY HANDS, YOU WERE CREATED IN MY IMAGE.
RISE, LET US LEAVE THIS PLACE, FOR YOU ARE IN ME AND I AM IN
YOU. TOGETHER WE FORM ONLY ONE PERSON AND WE CANNOT
BE SEPARATED.

— FROM AN ANCIENT HOMILY GIVEN ON EASTER EVE

ENDNOTES

Brennan Manning, "The Ragamuffin Gospel: Good News for the Bedraggled, Beat-Up, and Burnt Out" (Multnomah Books, 2005)

Keri Smith, "Finish This Book" (Perigee Trade, 2011)

Richard Rohr "Immortal Diamond: The Search for Our True Self" (Jossey-Bass, 2013)

Brene Brown, "Daring Greatly: How the Courage to Be Vulnerable Transforms the Way We Live, Love, Parent, and Lead" (Gotham, 2012)

Chip Conley, "Emotional Equations: Simple Truths for Creating Happiness + Success" (Free Press, 2012)

Richard Rohr, "Breathing Under Water: Spirituality and the Twelve Steps" (Franciscan Media, 2011)

Jud Wilhite, "Torn: Trusting God When Life Leaves You in Pieces" (Multnomah Books, 2011)

Bob Hamp, "Think Differently Live Differently: Keys to a Life of Freedom" (Thomas Nelson, 2011)

Viktor E. Frankl, "Man's Search For Meaning" (Beacon Press, 2006)

People of the Second Chance is dedicated to the radical restoration of lives every single day. We craft grace-based solutions in order to help people live an awesome life.

SecondChance.org
Contact@SecondChance.org
951-200-4123

1150 Crews Road, Suite G
Matthews, NC 28105

People of the Second Chance is a 501(c)(3) organization based in San Diego, CA.

YOU CAN BE COMFORTABLE OR COURAGEOUS, BUT YOU CANNOT BE BOTH.

FREEWAY

RECOMMENDED RESOURCES

LIFEPLAN

Take the next step to discovering your unique design and purpose. This one-on-one, two-day intensive experience will help you discover your core talents, clarify your mission, and put together a strategic LifePlan.
www.MikeFoster.tv

GRACENOMICS

Broken relationships, personal emptiness, and increasing disappointments in work and life prompt us to search out a new way of living. This book and group experience offers an innovative approach to surviving and thriving in our grace-starved society.
www.SecondChance.org/store

CORE STRENGTHS WORKSHOP

Gain awareness of your strengths and a deeper understanding of your core self. Experience a 1/2 day Core Strengths workshop and deploy your interpersonal strengths and own the results your choices produce.
www.CoreStrengths.com/events

FREEWAY FOUNDING PARTNERS

WITHOUT THE PASSIONATE COMMITMENT OF THE INDIVIDUALS BELOW,
FREEWAY WOULD NOT HAVE BEEN A REALITY!

Kevin and Robin Small

Bill and Andrea Townsend

Jud and Lori Wilhite

Mike and Laura Gogis

Peter and Jennifer McGowan

Shannon Sedgwick Davis

Greg and Laurel Spencer

Planet Ministries

In December of 2012, People of the Second Chance did a crowdsourcing fundraiser for the *Freeway* project. With a full and grateful heart we say, "Thank you" to those who gave generously to our campaign.

FREEWAY STRATEGIC PARTNERS

BriAnne Bellomy

Meeshee Scherrei

Jeff Shinabarger

Isaac Morford

David Miller

Jennifer May

Ashley Smith

Miss Mel

Chris Hull

Gabe Leadley

Scott Pace

Mohan Karulkar

Mary Lou & Larry Michalski

Adam Lorenz

Katie Vasquez

Kaleena Foster

LV Hanson

Jeffrey Espeseth

Scott Valentine

Scott Burns

Kenna Moore

Eileen Knowles

Mark Crosby

Katelyn Collison

Valley Fellowship

Kristen Martin

Kyle Stickens

Christopher Deitz

Scott Norlin

Mike Lehr

Tara Ghiatis

Jeremy Barr

Bryan Totten

XXXchurch

Dr. Melinda Gillies

Matthew Wood

Steve Graves

Darren Whitehead

Kyle and Debbie Kerekffy

Margaret Suehr

Nick Bradley

Karen Gach

Dominic Ellett

Clint Murray

Elisabeth Corcoran

Ashley Rose Little

Bill Green

Michael R. Nelson

Aggie Ansell

Jason Jaggard

Mike Rusch

Michael Conner

Bryce Green

Benjamin Moore

Jennifer White

Greg Darley

Gloria Enriquez

Louis Tagliaboschi

Mike Goldsworthy

Tracy Callison

Molly Sullivan

Carl David Flores

Jose Ceniceros

Eric Vancil

Tim Lemons

Sarah Caudill

Lindsay Coleman

THANK YOU...

Jason Jaggard for bringing your brilliance and for helping build every aspect of Freeway.

Tom Rinks for your friendship and creative pixie dust.

Scott Pace and the entire People of the Second Chance team.

Peter, Blake, Bryce, Carrie, and the amazing team at PlainJoe Studios.

Ryan, Caitlyn, Angela, and Annie for making the words and ideas so much better.

Josh Webb for adding your creative design and expertise.

David Hodges and Ryan O'Neal for your musical genius.

Nick Jones and Prolifik for helping us tell the story better.

Daley Hake for the photos.

Rachel, Michael, and Annie for your help with the video shoot.

The People of the Second Chance Board of Directors for being champions of grace.

Mike's small group, who shared their stories and shaped this project.

Bill Hybels, Anne Rand, Jorie Johnson and Willow Creek Community Church.

SPECIAL THANKS...

Jennifer, Jackson, and Taylor Foster for your love and support.

Bill Townsend for your wisdom and constant guidance.

Kevin and Robin Small for your constant belief and support and for being great neighbors.

Jud Wilhite for being the best friend a person could ever have.

Our family and friends who have cheered us on for so long.

And of course, the People of the Second Chance community.

NEXT STEPS FOR CHURCHES AND CHURCH LEADERS!

FREEWAY SERMON SERIES

The *Freeway* Sermon Series is a dynamic 6-8 week series designed to help your community connect to the God of second chances. This simple "turn-key" weekend series facilitates spiritual commitments, numeric growth and a passion for God's grace in your church. Contact us for more information.

FREEWAY CHURCH SMALL GROUPS

The *Freeway* workbook and the Group Discussion DVD were built specifically for church small groups. This highly engaging and strategically designed group experience facilitates life change, rich community and a more fulfilling walk with God. Contact us to learn how to implement *Freeway* groups in your church.

CONTACT US

951-200-4123

FREEWAY@SECONDCHANCE.ORG

SECONDCHANCE.ORG

OUR CHURCH RELATIONS TEAM IS READY TO HELP!
WE CAN ASSIST YOU WITH ANY OF YOUR QUESTIONS
AND OFFER EXCLUSIVE CHURCH DISCOUNTS.

Rescue Academy Live is a 2-day, intensive workshop designed to teach you the skills and strategies to help coach and counsel people. With our exclusive content and interactive learning format, *Rescue Academy Live* will unleash your passion to impact people's lives forever. The *Rescue Academy Live* workshop is facilitated by Mike Foster.

Rescue Academy is a 7-part online course to help transform you from an advice-giver to a life-giver. In this online academy you will learn how to positively impact friends, family and the people that you work with and develop your passion for helping people transform their lives.

Learn more at:
RescueAcademy.com

WONDER LIFE

A NOT-SO-PERFECT GUIDE TO WHO YOU ARE AND WHY YOU'RE HERE

Wonderlife: A Not-So-Perfect Guide to Who You Are and Why You're Here is a new small group resource and weekend series that takes people on an authentic journey through their not-so-perfect stories to find their sacred calling. The small group workbook, videos, and weekend series is based on the principles of Psalm 139 and demonstrates how God can take broken things and make them beautiful again. With stunning design and a common sense approach, Wonderlife is unlike any other curriculum on the market today.

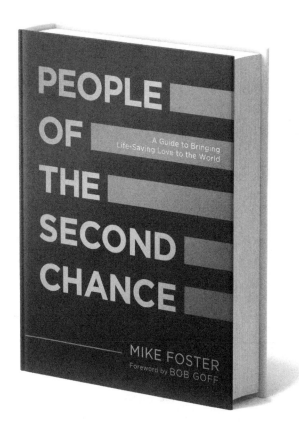

CALLING ALL IMPERFECTIONISTS AND HOPESTERS

People of the Second Chance: A Guide To Bringing Life-Saving Love To The World is the highly anticipated new book from Mike Foster that will stir a generation of imperfectionists to live as the beloved and throw prodigal parties. With the fierceness of a lion and the down-to-earth style of Mr. Rogers, this book will feel like an arousing pep-talk and a big warm hug.

Available wherever books are sold.

JOURNAL NOTES

JOURNAL NOTES

JOURNAL NOTES